SUCCESSFUL
NETWORKING

D0513107

SUCCESSFUL NETWORKING

HOW TO BUILD NEW NETWORKS FOR CAREER AND COMPANY PROGRESSION

FRANCES KAY

KoganPage

LONDON   PHILADELPHIA   NEW DELHI

Publisher's note

Every possible effort has been made to ensure that the information contained in this book is accurate at the time of going to press, and the publishers and author cannot accept responsibility for any errors or omissions, however caused. No responsibility for loss or damage occasioned to any person acting, or refraining from action, as a result of the material in this publication can be accepted by the editor, the publisher or the author.

First published in Great Britain and the United States in 2010 by Kogan Page Limited

120 Pentonville Road	525 South 4th Street, #241	4737/23 Ansari Road
London N1 9JN	Philadelphia PA 19147	Daryaganj
United Kingdom	USA	New Delhi 110002
www.koganpage.com		India

© Frances Kay, 2010

The right of Frances Kay to be identified as the author of this work has been asserted by her in accordance with the Copyright, Designs and Patents Act 1988.

ISBN   978 0 7494 5879 9
E-ISBN   978 0 7494 5915 4

British Library Cataloguing-in-Publication Data

A CIP record for this book is available from the British Library.

Library of Congress Cataloging-in-Publication Data

Kay, Frances, 1949–
    Successful networking : how to build new networks for career and company
progression / Frances Kay.
        p. cm.
    ISBN 978-0-7494-5879-9
    1. Career development. 2. Business networks. 3. Social networks.
4. Interpersonal relations. I. Title.
    HF5381.K39 2010
    650.1'3–dc22

                                                                        2009046000

Typeset by Graphicraft Limited, Hong Kong
Printed and bound in India by Replika Press Pvt Ltd

Dedication

To Patrick Forsyth and Neilson Kite, two of the
most generous people I know. Their innate ability to
network is impressive. Their achievements in their
respective careers are outstanding and proof that possessing
people skills makes a huge difference.

Contents

Publisher's note

All the case studies provided in the text are true and actually happened to people known to the author. The names in some cases have been changed.

Preface

The ability to network successfully is advantageous for anyone, young or old, experienced or fresh to the workplace. Everyone can network but it is amazing how many people either lack confidence or approach the task without much enthusiasm. Shyness and apathy are the two main barriers to success where 'people skills' are concerned. This book is designed to remove the fear factor and encourage you to make the effort to network for success. There are so many ways to do it, and it isn't difficult – you simply need to choose the method most suitable to your needs. The benefits are many: improving the chances of keeping your job, getting a new and better one, career progression, learning how to get along with others, improving personal effectiveness and company performance, to name but a few.

This book gives readers advice and guidance on handling any social or workplace situation that could be awkward. People are complex, and a lack of awareness of 'soft skills' can cause endless workplace challenges. Knowing that you have the ability to deal with all the challenges you might encounter will increase your self-confidence. The ability to network successfully has a powerful effect not only on the individual's performance but also on their organization's. This book also contains a lot of detailed information on the role of networking in the virtual community – essential knowledge for everyone today.

Networking, in virtual and physical terms, is a perennially popular subject. A book that teaches techniques and skills to get (and stay) ahead of the pack is useful for everyone at any stage in their working life. For those who feel daunted at the thought of networking, this book is vital reading. Why waste more time? Get ready to start making new contacts in the right way and find the right method for you.

About the author

Clients say of Frances Kay: 'She is unique in establishing and developing corporate networks and stakeholder relationships. In changing times, maintaining networks in physical and personal terms is of paramount importance. Her ability to take on this role in an intelligent manner is impressive. Frances represents organizations and individuals picking up and nurturing the threads of strategic business continuity.'

Frances acts as a consultant to specialist firms, assisting them in creating and establishing corporate networks and relationships for their business development. With many years' work experience covering politics, the diplomatic service and law, the majority of her time is now spent writing, researching, editing and giving talks based on her book topics. Frances has over 20 business books to her name. She is editor of *The Good Non-Retirement Guide 2010*, co-author with Patrick Forsyth of *Tough Tactics for Tough Times* and co-author with Neilson Kite of *Understanding NLP*, all published by Kogan Page. For further information see her website: www.franceskay.co.uk.

Tristan Kirby has worked for ten years in a problem solving and project management role with a leading blue chip company. He is experienced in business procedures and IT systems, including statistical analysis, business development and customer relationship management. He is a Master's graduate in War, Violence, Security and International Relations and is an active research consultant contributing to various texts on business and political matters. He has also worked as a journalist and speech writer and enjoyed a brief career as a professional musician touring internationally with a rock band.

Introduction

Human beings, by changing the inner attitudes of their minds, can change the outer aspects of their lives.

William James (1842–1910)

Networking: it's a word that means many things to people. What actually is it? What's it for? What sort of people network? Why do they bother? 'People skills': are they something that can be acquired? Or are you born with them? What do skilled networkers have to offer – other than an impressive ability for self-publicity?

This book will attempt to answer some of these questions and provide suggestions and hints for those for whom networking doesn't come naturally. It will also explain the many benefits of networking, inside and outside the workplace, person to person and virtual networking. In essence, networking is a huge asset to anyone who wishes to succeed personally or professionally. The most powerful and influential people are usually keen networkers who have innumerable contacts. They have grown so adept at doing it, it's really second nature to them. But they have probably been working at it for a long time.

Some keen amateurs who decide to take up networking do so with the greatest enthusiasm. They start by trying to get to know the entire world, contacting everyone they meet. Within a very short time they boast that they have thousands of 'close friends' in their network – each of whom they can call to mind easily when necessary. Of course, in the virtual world this is exactly what happens – you can instantly become best friends with a huge group of people. However, it could be awkward if all those people decided to make a personal visit to you at the same time.

Networking with the entire world, although technically possible, isn't really helpful. Networking – or relationship building; call it what you will – is more than anything else a personal thing. Each person has a unique circle of acquaintances, friends and confidants. The best thing to do is to start small and get a bit of confidence first. The purpose is not to fawn over the rich and famous – they're the first to spot phoneys, and are good at avoiding audacious opportunists. Effective networking is best done slowly; give it time.

Don't think you're a failure if you haven't made six new friends by the time you reach your workplace each morning. Exchanging contact details with total strangers is not what it's about – unless of course you've just been involved in a traffic accident and it's a requirement of the law. The ideal way is to find a connection point with another person and take it from there.

Many books have been written about networking and the art of making friends. There are constant references to it in the media, and the internet has had a phenomenal impact on the world of networking; in this book there is a whole section on networking in the virtual world. Right now, networking is the skill to have if you wish to succeed, and the virtual community is waiting to welcome you. There are 'new' virtual methods being discovered and innovative systems regularly being developed. But the curious thing is, there's nothing new about networking at all: Dale Carnegie published his first book about it in 1937 – though even he probably didn't invent it. Making friends probably started in a cave somewhere...

Whatever stage you have reached in your life or career, you cannot afford *not* to network. It is a fact but not everyone realizes it or knows what to do about it. Being a successful networker will mean that you can confidently build rapport with others; create your own vibrant network of contacts; be strategic and focused about doing it; keep close to your existing clients and find new ones.

For those who hate the idea, think it a waste of effort or are so terrified they would rather visit the dentist than meet new people, this book will throw you a lifeline. It will help you to get started, virtually or physically, without feeling much pain, and convince you of the long-term benefits of relationship building. Don't waste another minute or lose out on any opportunities that come your way – read *Successful Networking*.

1

Confidence and motivation to network

A positive attitude may not solve all your problems, but it will annoy enough people to make it worth the effort.

Herm Allbright (1876–1944)

A large number of successful professionals today believe that 'who you know' is just as important as 'what you know'. You may, for a number of reasons, be doubtful or sceptical about that statement. If you're unsure, this book sets out to persuade you otherwise. Doing business certainly relies as much on people skills as on qualifications and experience. You may find it more difficult to achieve the success you deserve if your skills set is unbalanced – loads of one and not much of the other. No matter how brilliant you are at your job, if you want to get ahead, good connections do help. Working away for hours on end at your desk in splendid isolation isn't enough – unless you're networking in the virtual community, of course. Getting to know people and making new contacts is an essential part of working effectively: the right attitude really matters.

Key point

There are four core qualities that will help you become a successful networker: curiosity, generosity, confidence and motivation. Without any of these you will find it an uphill task.

People do mean business, and most people are much happier working with those they like – or those they recognize as having similarities to themselves. The main reasons people build personal and professional networks are for career and corporate success. Your organization will stand out ahead of its competitors and your promotional prospects will be enhanced if you have a vibrant network of contacts and friends. These are two hugely motivational factors. One important thing to remember at this introductory stage: it helps to be curious about other people. They will find you far more interesting if you show an interest in them. Why should this be? The simple answer is that most people enjoy talking about themselves. Keep this firmly in mind when meeting new people – the art of networking is not just about *you*.

Now that jobs for life are a thing of the past, building your own network is even more important. Workers switch roles and careers far more frequently than they used to. There's a growing generation that has specialized in portfolio careers and transferable skills. This is proven by the increasing number of entrepreneurs and consultants who set up businesses (usually in a sector of which they have experience or in which they enjoy working). If you want further encouragement, 765 of the richest 1,000 people in Britain and Ireland in 2009 were self-made millionaires (*The Sunday Times Rich List 2009*, published 26 April 2009). Anyone setting up a business for themself needs good contacts; acquiring networking skills is essential. If you're not an entrepreneur but are employed or looking for work, personal recommendations speak volumes and are often more persuasive than the best-presented CV.

Developing a successful network isn't just about getting to know people you don't already know. Don't forget about the others – the ones you already know or have known a long time. Family, friends and acquaintances from school, college or university can all be part of your unique network. Current and former colleagues should also be included in your circle. Another important group are members of your industry association or profession. Finally, don't exclude the competition. Many a potential rival has been turned into a valuable ally by means of effective interpersonal skills. Being generous and courteous to others makes you memorable and is a great networking asset.

As with many things, those who are confident and have extrovert characteristics find physical (as opposed to virtual) networking less difficult than those who are timid or self-effacing. Some people are natural-born networkers and have loads of charisma. For others, who want to network face to face, the skills have to be learned. This is not difficult if you use some tried and tested methods, which will be described in detail further on in the book. One of these worth mentioning at the outset is the ability to be flexible. Everyone is familiar with the saying 'If you do what you've always done, you'll get what you've always got.' The same approach over and over again in networking will not yield results. And why should it? No one is the same as another person – so why should repeating the same introductory remarks and conversational opening gambits be right for each contact, let alone each occasion? Become confident and adept at trying new approaches and you will succeed. Finding the appropriate way to further a business relationship-building process is an important skill. There are many methods to choose and ringing the changes from time to time is vital. Once you get used to networking and begin to make progress with relationship building, the motivation to carry on is high.

Key point

If you're wondering whether networking is worth the effort, the answer is a resounding 'Yes'. But getting good results isn't quick. That's why confidence and motivation levels need to be healthy and sustained.

At its best, networking can give you access to unpublished information. People will give their opinions on matters – in person and online – that you can't get from websites, publications and advertising materials. Just as you might ask a friend where the best restaurant is, people are usually willing to talk about their work. If you show an interest, they may offer to help. Networking requires generosity – giving rather than taking. Even if you cannot directly help someone who has helped you, there may be an indirect way: someone you know may be useful to them and you could introduce them.

By developing and nurturing a strong network of personal contacts, you can become more effective in business and help your career to progress. The main reasons why it works are:

■ The greater your range of contacts, the more career opportunities you will have.
■ Good relationships in the workplace will be helpful when taking charge of new situations.
■ Strong personal networks mean higher job satisfaction.
■ Problems can be solved faster, before they become crises, because of access to a number of possible solution providers.
■ Greater access to information (employment, industry sector etc).
■ Increased collaborative opportunities with others.
■ The chance to develop long-term professional relationships.

Remember – it's reciprocal. This is where the generosity factor comes in: if you help others, they will help you in return.

How to get started

I do not believe that friends are necessarily the people you like best; they are merely the ones who got there first.
                              Peter Ustinov (1921–2004) (*Dear Me*)

You may be wondering where on earth you go from here. It probably feels much more daunting than it is. Developing relationships, whether socially or at work, is all about rapport building. If you're someone who is naturally people-aware, then you probably make connections easily and quickly.

In fact, networking and building relationships with people are something everyone does on a daily basis with varying degrees of success. Most people use a computer and send e-mails. This is a way of networking – it's online, it's virtual, you don't have to get out of your chair. However, getting on the bus to go to work or going into a shop brings you into physical contact with new people. There's nothing unusual about this or particularly risky. But it is potential networking. Being able to interact with others in a relaxed and easy way is well within anyone's capabilities. Those who enjoy it (meeting people face to face or using the internet) find that it's fun. For those who don't enjoy it – and there are plenty who fall into this category – networking is the best way to overcome shyness, discover unexpected opportunities and break down the barriers to increasing their circle of friends and contacts.

Before going too much further, here are the main reasons why it is advantageous to network successfully:

▓   to realize your full potential;
▓   to succeed in making new friendships;

- ■ to gain more self-confidence;
- ■ to form new business relationships;
- ■ to find opportunities to give and to receive;
- ■ to have an advantage over people who can't, won't or don't want to network.

Reluctant though you may be to take the first tentative steps, whether from fear, apathy or lack of time, a positive outlook is vital to successful relationship building. Once you learn how to do it in a way that suits you, you will overcome shyness, get excited about it and find you do have the time. Once you've broken down the barriers that have prevented you trying up to now, you'll feel completely different. You will gain in confidence because you have worked out the best way to network for you – remember, it requires a genuine curiosity about others. You need to be interested rather than interesting. When you are generous to those you meet, you will find the motivation to create personal opportunities through your positive mental attitude.

You can make more friends in two months by becoming interested in other people than you can in two years by trying to get other people interested in you.

Dale Carnegie

And there you have it, the key to this whole networking business; in a word: *curiosity*. As you read on, you will find that, rather than killing the cat, curiosity is actually just what's needed to get you started.

Curiosity pays dividends in the art of making friends. Those of you who have natural curiosity will know what I mean. Perhaps you can recall an occasion when you overcame your instincts and spoke to someone you didn't know, and which had a beneficial outcome. For example, when you next attend a business event where there is a guest speaker, you might ask a question in the Q&A session. If you are brave enough to do this, you will find that people come up to you at the networking session afterwards and talk to you. Why is this?

The first reason is that you'll have shown curiosity – an interest in what the speaker said. You will have listened and probably learned something you didn't know. Second, people react with curiosity towards you because you've made the effort to speak out. They become interested because they might be even more reserved than you are, and wish they'd found the courage to raise their hand. Their interest might range from saying that they were just about to ask the same question themselves; or perhaps they wish to discuss the answer the speaker gave you. They might have agreed with the question you asked or they might not. But they will show interest in who you are, what you do and why you felt moved to ask a question in the first place.

Asking questions is easy to do if you're going to be doing a lot of your networking virtually. There are loads of different ways of asking questions via the internet: such as posting a question on a website forum, or in a chat room, or by blogging. Any of these should generate interest from other people.

Nerves and apathy – two great inhibitors to networking

Case study

James was a whiz with figures. He loved preparing analyses, reports, graphs, charts and diagrams showing the growth rate of the financial products of his company. He had been doing his job for a number of years and was successful but he knew he was stuck at his present level. He was midway up the managerial ladder and wanted promotion so that he could achieve his desired career goal. Unfortunately, James was not naturally gregarious. His brilliance at his job did not help him in the slightest. His colleagues hardly knew him, they had limited appreciation of his work and generally thought he was aloof. When James's director suggested coaching to unlock his potential, he reluctantly agreed.

It was shyness that was holding him back. James wanted to be able to mix with people, but felt he wasn't any good at it. Because he was nervous he didn't try to overcome his fear, so it built up an even greater barrier to climb. The coach encouraged James to pay attention to people who he thought were good mixers and take note of what they did. After a few coaching sessions James announced that he'd 'got it' and explained how this had happened. He'd been standing next to his wife in the supermarket queue as she started a conversation with a complete stranger. He realized suddenly that because she was a naturally curious person she talked to people wherever she happened to be. She was always making new friends and coming home with extraordinary bits of information. James practised this method of talking to complete strangers outside the workplace until he built up enough confidence to try it out at work. It made a huge difference to him and to his colleagues' perception of him. The result was that shortly afterwards he was offered a more senior position with his company.

Case study

Not long ago, Saira was due to attend a meeting for which she had no enthusiasm whatsoever. It was a boiling hot summer evening in London and she was tired after a long day at work. When Saira arrived at the venue, matters got worse. The air conditioning in the conference suite was broken – it was stifling. Everyone was hot and flustered – she nearly walked out. What was the point of staying in such an atmosphere when she had no desire to do so and felt that no positive benefit could possibly result?

However, as she'd travelled some way to reach the conference venue she decided to stay. She found the first seat available and sat down, without looking round. The man sitting next to her turned and asked if she would like him to fetch her a glass of water. When he returned they struck up a conversation and discovered they had both attended the same school for a time and had a number of mutual friends. The result? A friendship began, and the bonus was a great new working relationship. This chance meeting and subsequent business opportunity could so easily have been missed if apathy had won the day and Saira had gone home instead of staying.

Setting goals

But what if you don't want to improve your self-esteem? What's going to make you get up, take notice and climb out of your safe haven? One way is to show that there is a clear connection between dreams and goals; that self-imposed barriers and limits can be broken and life will change. Didn't The Beatles write a song about getting by with a little help from your friends? They must have known a thing or two about networking. But consider the opposite viewpoint for a moment. A couple of centuries ago a famous British diplomat decided to pursue a course of international action which became known as 'the policy of Splendid Isolation'. The idea was that in order to avoid trouble or disagreements, it was best not to talk to anybody. It worked along the lines of 'If you have no friends, you'll have no enemies.'

Actually, when put into practice, this whole premise is fatally flawed. It not only had hideous consequences for his country as a whole in both the national and international arenas, it was disastrous for his own career. This policy certainly didn't prevent other countries picking quarrels or being difficult. On the contrary, it positively encouraged them. The essential point to note is that without any friends or allies, you can appear to be weak and helpless. In terms of international diplomacy it was a complete calamity. It is worth thinking about in a networking context. If you believe that isolating yourself from others seems like a form of protection, in reality it doesn't prevent others from attacking you. What's worse, you have no reserves or support framework when you most need it. You have a back-up system on your computer network, which means your work is protected. Wouldn't it be wise to create a back-up system for your professional and social life too?

Key point

If you make an effort to like people, it is harder for them to dislike you. Extending the hand of friendship is a great way to start. When you have friends, life is more enjoyable.

So where do you start in creating or reviving your own (physical or online) personal network? Don't say you haven't got one, because everyone has. Some people may not believe it. Whether you realize it or not, it is important to pay attention to it, work on it and use it to advantage. It's unique, like you. It contains a wealth of individuals, information and opportunity.

Opportunity is missed by most people because it is dressed in overalls and looks like work.

Thomas A Edison (1847–1931)

If those people you'd like to remember you do so favourably the next time you meet, the possible rewards are endless. Building relationships takes time. Bear in mind that you can hurry tasks, but people can't be rushed. People also respond well to commitment and effort, so be focused, self-disciplined and patient. If people like you, they will be happy to help you. It's as simple as that.

Why not have a go at networking? Set yourself a personal goal to increase your contacts. It could be something as simple as speaking to one total stranger each day for just a week and sending two online messages a day. This might sound ridiculous, but it takes a lot of courage to talk to a random person if you're not keen on the idea, just as you probably don't want to send out 'cold' enquiries by e-mail.

But you probably do need the practice, so whether you make a success or mess up, it won't matter at this stage. You're not expected to end up with seven new friends at the end of the first week, or to have clinched several new deals for your company via computer. You are simply attempting to overcome the mental block of physically meeting people you don't know and engaging strangers in a virtual conversation.

In case you need a few more reasons for building relationships, let's look at some R words.

Relationships: why build them? Several reasons: because people can't live without friendships; because isolation is an unnatural state; because successful people usually have a wide range of contacts.

Recognition: isn't it nice to go somewhere and meet familiar faces? Someone giving you a wave or a smile in the middle of a group of strangers is a big confidence boost. You'll instantly feel better.

Recall: if you can remember some particular detail about the person you're meeting for the second time, you'll rise high in their estimation. It can be as simple as enquiring about their recent holiday, their family or new job.

Reaction: one of the things you want to aim for is a positive reaction when you encounter them again.

Respect: get it right and you'll gain their trust. The ability to show respect for others is what will help you gain their respect.

Responsibility: if you take responsibility for your relationships, it will mean that you'll be in control of your personal network. It's worth a lot to you – so don't be careless with it.

Confidence-building techniques

My mother used to say that there are no strangers, only friends you haven't met yet. She's now in a maximum-security twilight home in Australia.

Dame Edna Everage (Barry Humphries)

Sceptical though you may be about networking, it can change your life. You may not believe it yet but it doesn't matter how clever you are, what your background is, whether you're a man or a woman, if you're tall, short, fat, thin, beautiful or not, or how old you are. People are more confident and successful the better connected they are. This applies both in business as well as personally, physically and virtually. With growing confidence you will be able to develop new friends or relationships, and so it goes on.

Key point

When I once asked an audience what they felt about networking, almost all of them said that they found walking into a room full of strangers absolutely terrifying. One person helpfully added that he was actually more scared of death, which did put matters slightly into perspective.

If on a scale of 1 to 10, you would grade your dislike of networking anywhere from 6 or above, you should try to work out why you're so anti it. Whether your fear has reached phobic proportions or not, you aren't alone. Many thousands of people – young and old, experienced or not – find networking scary and stressful. But once you've done a little preparation, you should be able to take the first few tentative steps into the unknown with confidence. If it isn't fear but apathy that's holding you back, you need only a few small successes to get you fired up with enthusiasm and confidence. If it's lack of time, you will begin to make time for it once you've seen what a difference it can make.

Key point

Developing relationships, whether at work or outside work, is really about overcoming reluctance – be that shyness, lack of interest or being too busy. Putting other people before yourself – that's the best way to start, and it builds self-confidence.

Do you know someone who is naturally people-aware? These lucky individuals make connections easily and quickly. Their contacts and friends are plentiful and physically meeting new people is no great ordeal. If you are shy or reticent, you may feel a bit disadvantaged at first, but don't worry. These soft skills can be acquired and, with a little practice, they'll become second nature. One useful tip is to watch charismatic people when they're in action. When an opportunity presents itself, you could possibly suggest that they let you shadow them at a business event or two. Don't take this too literally, though. Shadowing doesn't involve hiding behind pillars or potted palms, pretending you are an espionage agent, or skulking around the sides of the room looking furtive. Any of that sort of behaviour and at best you will appear odd and get some strange glances. At worst, you'll be escorted from the event by the security people for gate-crashing.

Ways to increase motivation

Business success is twenty per cent strategy, eighty per cent people.
John Sunderland, former chairman of Cadbury Schweppes

Not long ago a client wrote a referral letter for me, which said, 'She is unique in establishing and developing corporate networks and relationships. In changing times maintaining networks in physical and personal terms is of paramount importance. Frances's ability to take on this role in an intelligent manner is impressive, representing organizations or individuals, picking up and nurturing the threads of strategic business continuity.'

Impressive? This was an unsolicited testimonial and made pleasant reading. Do you ever ask people what they think about you? What qualities and attributes best describe you? Maybe a little 360° feedback would help. Positive remarks from other people are the best motivational boost. Because you may not be convinced by this networking stuff you'd never ask, would you? You probably think that people haven't noticed you, let alone know who you are. They probably do know you, and they'll certainly have opinions about you and the work you do. Aren't you just a tiny bit curious what people think about you? What qualities and attributes would they say best describe you? Of course, if you weren't so disinterested or shy, you'd be brave enough to initiate a little bit of feedback. If you did, you'd be agreeably surprised at what you heard.

Key point

Successful networkers put people first – they are the most important ingredient of all. The core attributes required are enquiring, listening, researching and organizing.

Here's a useful mnemonic about nurturing relationships. To network successfully you need to be able to build RAPPORT:

R   relationships
A   are
P   powerful,
P   providing
O   opportunities and
R   rewards
T   today.

Rapport building requires skill. The key is to develop a genuine and sincere interest in other people. As mentioned earlier in this chapter, in its simplest form this means being curious. It involves getting to know people and offering to introduce them to others with whom they may have a common interest. This is a habit well worth cultivating because it brings untold opportunities which you might otherwise miss. Also, coincidences can and do occur with increasing frequency – all of which adds interest to exchanges with others inside or outside the working environment.

2

Finding the right networks

Never refuse any advance of friendship, for if nine out of ten bring you nothing, one alone may repay you.

Madame Claudine Alexandrine Guérin de Tencin
(1682–1749)

One of the interesting things about networking is that even if you don't realize it, you do have a network already. It most certainly exists, even though you may not consciously cultivate it. Your network includes your family and friends, neighbours and their contacts. It includes your work colleagues at all levels (upwards as well as downwards) and all their contacts. It includes the support staff who work in your organization (career advisers, librarians, human resources professionals, training and development professionals). In addition, there are former work colleagues and members of the professional bodies, or other clubs or associations to which you belong (these may be related to work or social activities). Sometimes it is easy to forget the people you encounter at conferences, courses and other events, but they should also be added. Some of your competitors could be usefully included in your network. They may seem at first glance to offer similar services or products to yours but they might help provide a solution by delivering extended services which could make your clients even happier. Turning competitors into trusted associates is another form of networking. Finally, there are the members of your online discussion groups, social networking sites and other internet-based community chat rooms, blogs and twitters.

If all of this sounds overwhelming, there is an important reason why you really ought to network. If you are not out and about talking to people, or networking online, you can bet that others are. Whether you are looking for new opportunities for business or a new position, or to increase your social clout, you do need to be visible – in physical and virtual terms. If you don't maintain a presence and keep your (or your company's) visibility high, don't be surprised if you are overtaken by others who are more proactive. They will capture the attention and reap rewards that could have been yours.

Key point

When your network is established and working for you, you will appear to advantage within, as well as outside, your organization.

The right network for you (particularly if you are new to the idea and need a bit of encouragement) is the one in which you operate most comfortably. When learning to swim, people usually start in the shallow end and work their way gradually into deeper water. The same rule applies with networking. You should try to seize every opportunity to develop your network, because you never know when a contact might be valuable or you can offer help to them. But you don't have to do it all in the same week. Take advantage of any invitations to seminars, meetings and conferences. Join online groups that are looking for new members, particularly if you already know someone who belongs to them.

These can include physical groups – professional bodies, staff associations and networks, unions or clubs associated with social and sporting activities or groups in the virtual community. Many people network effectively online and this is one area where it is very simple to increase your contacts – at the press of a button. No need to get your coat on, you don't have to leave your chair.

Deciding on your networking strategy

When making a start, like many things it's a good idea to keep things simple. Take it slowly and see how you get on.

You can develop any network you want, but it will need to be flexible and adaptable because your objectives will change as you go along. You can focus on social networking and include business and career development.

The meeting of two personalities is like the contact of two chemical substances: if there is any reaction, both are transformed.
Carl Jung (1875–1961)

Personal social networks are a good place to start, because they are less scary and slightly easier to generate. The people you'll be meeting do not have quite the same power to affect your life as those in the work environment. By the time you've grown in confidence, and experience, you can start on the professional networks you may wish to develop (which require more advanced skills) with greater ease.

Before going much further, if you already have a list of contacts, in whatever form, review it to see if it is user friendly, effective and current. This may involve you in a lot of scrabbling around for bits of paper or old business cards stuffed in desk drawers. There are many people whose filing systems are less than perfect. Perhaps you loathe clutter and you have an expertly filled database, an electronic diary and an e-mail address book brimming with details of your entire network neatly displayed at the touch of a button. Whichever it is, consider the following questions. Do you communicate regularly with those in your own network? Do you proactively seek to increase and refresh your contacts? Do you do this formally or is it an informal arrangement? Do you ever ask your contacts for help or offer support and advice to them? Do you pay attention to your network, keeping it in good shape for easy access and management?

Key point

Networks work best according to the amount of give and take. You only get out of them what you are prepared to put in.

Keeping your eye on the ball (players)

Remember that networking is flexible, so you can develop contacts internally, externally, upwards as well as downwards, virtually and physically. The purpose of building good relationships within your company is to be well informed. This saves valuable time and increases productivity. You also pick up on internal politics and are able to maximize opportunities that come your way. Externally, you will have valuable contacts who act as referrers, bridges, sources, links and influencers to help you achieve your personal goals. Look upwards if you can. If you are able to cultivate a number of influential people, this can be very rewarding. A good example is if you are interested in networking for fundraising for a charity. Bear in mind that the people you will want to contact are usually busy and it may not be easy to reach them. Finally, don't forget that it's not only people in high places who can be useful to you. Often a key piece of information may be known to the unlikeliest of individuals. It is unwise to ignore someone just because they do not hold a very senior position.

Identifying key players is an essential skill. Influential people are not necessarily those in high places. If you have a wide range of contacts you will find that some people who are not in powerful positions of seniority can wield considerable power.

Movers and shakers usually far exceed the boundaries of their office positions. They make it their business to see and be seen. Identify them among your contacts. They are important to keep track of – you never know where they are going to turn up next.

Corporate citizens are the hard-working, non-political types, who are great resources for information and advice. They usually know the inside and outside of their business, their department and most personnel. If you nurture them and seek their advice when appropriate they could be invaluable. Better to ask them first than later wish that you had.

Where do you want this to lead?

Obviously you want it to result in success. Here are some ways in which individuals in different companies invested time and effort in building the right connections, and the various outcomes they achieved.

Introductions. A newly formed IT-based company wanted to find potential investors. They worked hard to develop a network of business connections to help them source potential funders. They spent six months researching suitable prospects, influencers and connectors, to identify a number of venture capitalists and investors. From a number of introductions they found three venture capitalists who were prepared to help them. They now have sufficient investment for their growth over the next five years. Their business is on track to perform to its maximum potential.

Alliances. An international firm of consulting engineers wanted to improve their ability to win more business in the UK and Europe. Their business development strategy was drawn up to increase their links with, and standing among, the most relevant movers and shakers in the construction and property industry. By working hard to raise their profile within their profession, they nurtured influencers and recommenders who helped them build strong strategic alliances. As a result they were awarded a number of significant construction awards and several internationally acclaimed projects.

Customer relationship management. A high-profile practice of UK architects carried out a client satisfaction survey to benchmark their reputation. They compiled questionnaires, interviewed a selection of clients, prospects and influencers. The results reflected the company's strengths and identified areas where improvement was necessary. By following up on some of the encouraging comments received, the directors were able to acquire repeat business and extension work that increased their annual turnover by almost 20 per cent.

Team building. A charity had to organize a high-profile fundraiser at a time when there were a number of other similar events. Apathy had set in, take-up on tables was slow and ticket sales were sluggish. The organizers needed to harness energy and enthuse staff to take the project forward. By calling in favours from some of the charity's high-profile patrons and supporters, it was possible to rekindle enthusiasm and energize volunteers. A brainstorming session took place among a group of individuals who had diverse skills and personality types. A number of new initiatives were suggested. Everyone took on a role that best suited their personal strengths. The result: the project went forward with eagerness because volunteers worked harmoniously and productively together and the event was a sell-out.

Succession planning. A financial corporation needed to help some of their executives who were on track for career progression. Although successful within the organization, a number of these individuals had been appraised as being highly task-aware. Due to their lack of awareness of the importance of personal contacts within the company and weak interpersonal skills, their promotion prospects were on hold.

The company looked within itself and, through its internal network, identified several key individuals who were asked to become mentors for these young managers. By setting up a mentoring and coaching programme, the company was able to help them back on track. Their interpersonal skills increased, they became less task-aware and in addition the company gained the advantage of smoothing its succession planning.

Suggestions for not wasting time

I always like to know everything about my new friends, and nothing about my old ones.

Oscar Wilde (1854–1900)

If you are apprehensive about the networking process, you'll find it more than easy to justify not doing it. You can probably think of lots of valid reasons for avoiding social contact – but they're not reasons. They are actually excuses: 'Can't get there on time', 'I'm really busy that day', 'Surely someone else can go', 'I'll do it next week/month/year'. Many people faced with doing something they dislike swiftly turn into the world's most accomplished procrastinators. This won't get you anywhere, let alone off the starting grid. It's best, if you can, to take stock of the situation honestly and do an appraisal. Here are some suggestions on how to do just that.

Be analytical. Understand the emotional cycle: Ask yourself which situations and what occasions make you most nervous. Make a list and study recurring themes and triggers. Is it, for example, that all-too-common fear of walking into a room full of strangers? If so, start networking online.

Self-esteem inventory. Build yourself up you so that you start believing you can do it. You will manage to have a conversation with someone you've never met before. Once you've done it, it will be a positive experience.

Visualize your success. Use your imagination and picture yourself in an animated exchange with a really attractive or interesting person, having a great online conversation with someone who is fun and which results in a win–win situation.

Attributes that generate success. Behave and look as though you already have the confidence you desire. Good posture and presentation help. Use positive words and phrases and speak in a confident manner. In virtual networking, choose words and phrases carefully and don't write anything that could cause embarrassment if it ended up in the wrong in-box.

Attitude and judgements about others. Never mind the packaging – look inside the box to see what's there. Don't allow yourself to make hasty and precipitate judgements for entirely the wrong reasons about people you've just connected with. Try to suspend reaction and take the more measured view.

Breaking new ground. Stepping into the unknown is where it starts. If you do what you've always done, you'll get what you've always got. So take a deep breath and make yourself do it.

Make that first impression count: Deep breath, relax, smile – and go for it.

Key point

The best way to start is by just being yourself. This takes away a lot of stress and pressure about trying to make yourself appear something you're not.

Time and patience are required but straight away you will start connecting with new people and enjoying new activities. With an open mind and a flicker of interest (or a spirit of adventure, if you're getting the hang of this) you could expand your horizons infinitely further than you'd first thought. When networking in the virtual community, the world is at your fingertips. In physical and geographical terms, you may have the opportunity to sign up for some foreign trips. Anything like this would increase your network and your outlook. There's no point in limiting yourself to one particular method or area. If you are prepared to try the direct approach (face-to-face contact as opposed to the online method) this can be done by chance or by design.

You could arrange to go out regularly, say once a week, to a place where you feel safe and comfortable. If you like keeping fit, the local sports club or fitness centre is a great place to start. If you play competitive sport, teams usually comprise more than one person. The best advice is to be proactive. Nothing will happen if you don't make an effort. Wherever you begin, your first success will probably be in the most unexpected place and at the least anticipated time.

Do not protect yourself by a fence, but rather by your friends.

Czech proverb

If you are happy pursuing casual methods of meeting new people, what about when travelling? Whether it is your daily commute, travelling to work by bus or train, or at the airport if your job involves international travel, these could all provide great opportunities for networking. Considering the unreliability of many means of transport, you could well be subjected to delays. While you stand in a queue or wait patiently at the airport, station or bus stop, why not use the time to strike up a conversation with someone who looks interesting? 'It pays to talk,' the BT advertisement told us in the 1980s. With the growth in mobile technology, fewer people talk when waiting around; most are connected by virtual means and have their eyes glued to a laptop or a PDA (personal digital assistant: basically a handheld or palmtop computer). Don't waste this time, use it to increase your online network.

Case study

Jan was on holiday in a European capital city and had been visiting its famous museums. He was in one building looking at the architecture when a man approached him and asked if he was interested in going to see an exhibition and attend a lecture. He explained that a friend of his had been unavoidably detained and wouldn't be able to use his ticket. Learning that Jan was interested in the lecture because he was a student of the subject, the man gladly gave him his spare ticket. He introduced himself and was very knowledgeable about the subject under discussion. After the lecture the two had supper together and a good friendship began.

One of the simplest and most effective ways of meeting new people on your own territory is by entertaining at home. This is good for students and people on a tight budget. You could throw a party and invite a few of your friends to bring a guest with them, someone you don't know. If you invite six friends and each brings a guest they know but you don't, your circle of acquaintances will grow. Repeat this four times a year and you'll have a great network in a fairly short space of time. The other advantage is that if you are nervous about meeting new people, there is already a connection here – your mutual friend. Don't worry if you can't cook. Tell people it's 'bring and share'; this takes the strain off the host or hostess.

You could get involved with a not-for-profit organization and invest your time and energy as a volunteer, or by participating in fundraising events. The more involved you become in whatever voluntary work you do, the better you'll get to know others who share your interest and desire to 'make a difference'. You will be far more enthusiastic about working as a volunteer if you have passion for the cause. Whatever your passion – from bee keeping to xylophone playing – there is an activity for you where you could make new friends.

Many organizations offer volunteer opportunities but some of these require a serious time commitment. Take into consideration that you will not be paid, and select which charity you wish to support with great care. Charities and special-interest groups are a fantastic way to connect with like-minded people and most of them depend on their dedicated teams of volunteers, without whom they could not provide the services they offer. There are huge personal rewards for helping in this way. You'll experience a genuine feeling of self-worth and real usefulness. If you've not been that fortunate in making friends and feeling welcome, this is of immense value and has a really positive effect on your self-esteem. Do try this if you're not sure of the benefits of networking or are recovering from previous bad experiences or difficult personal times.

Perhaps the most obvious place to start networking is at work. Sometimes, because you see the same people every day, familiarity blinds you to the fact that they could become friends. People who work together get to know each other's habits over a long period of time. If a colleague is unfailingly cheerful and good-humoured between nine and five, it's unlikely they will turn into a morose and depressed individual outside the office. Some companies have a good number of social events you can take part in.

Given the many different types of people there are in the world, some of us have definite ideas as to what sort of people we like and where they may be found. There is so much opportunity and variety in the different methods and approaches to meeting new people, you'll be spoiled for choice. Try to mix the methods you use, because this will optimize your chances of success, you'll build confidence faster and be able to judge which feels right for you. Make use of the opportunity to visit new and interesting places, and then meeting people along the way will be a bonus.

Once you start on this process it will become easier for you to identify people with whom you have common interests, and with whom friendships may develop. Bear in mind that some people will be less keen to make friends. You may want to take it slowly and develop a few contacts over the long term. Whatever you do, make sure you feel comfortable doing it.

3

Networking groups

Eighty per cent of success is just turning up.

Woody Allen

Whether you are learning about networking or are an experienced hand at it, the advice in this chapter relates to the various kinds of networking groups that operate. If you are looking for advice on how to network on line, the next chapter deals specifically with networking in the virtual community, while this chapter is about face-to-face networking.

Key point

Networking is essential for building internal and external contacts. Inside the organization it fosters relationships with superiors, staff and peers, and outside with customers, suppliers and competitors.

In brief, internal networking is something the HR department or personnel office need to utilize to stay on top of current events within the organization. It gives them up-to-date information on the status and performance of employees and provides current feedback on company strategy. Internal networking is seen by some as just being friendly and working as a team to get the job done. However, HR departments that communicate regularly with each division in an organization can easily observe staff motivation levels. They do this by observing employee turnover and which departments or sections are lacking support or missing deadlines. This enables them to detect the overall health of the company. Effective internal networks in organizations help management to come up with ideas or solutions to achieve business goals and objectives.

> *Call it a clan, call it a network, call it a tribe, call it a family. Whatever you call it, whoever you are, you need one.*
>
> Jane Howard

One of the reasons why networking gets a bad name is because people who do not understand the process abuse it – by trying to sell services or products. Meeting people who do not respect your values and attitudes, who have poor interpersonal skills and who find it difficult to share, can be off-putting. If you've encountered these types at networking events, they tend to be obsessed with themselves or their company's product or services, and show little if any curiosity about others. They miss the point of networking entirely by trying to dominate groups and conversations. They don't engage in dialogue or show any interest in offering help to those they meet.

There are lots of business and professional associations and other organizations that offer networking opportunities. Should you already know a bit about it but have fallen into a networking rut, these ideas may help you expand your network. Try to attend networking events on a regular basis so that you get to know people and they get to know you. It pays to focus on ways to expand your network. Whether you are building a network locally, nationally or internationally, the aim should be to make yourself visible and valuable to others.

Key point

Whether you are a self-employed professional or ambitious to succeed in your company, industry or sector, the 'need to know' and the 'need to be known by' are essential business skills.

Business networking groups meet on a regular basis – usually weekly or monthly. They are set up with networking as the main intention. They include people from a variety of professions and industry sectors. The meetings take place at breakfast or lunch or after work. Some groups have a structured format, such as a detailed timetable and programme with guest speakers or special topics. Others may have a more informal mix-and-mingle arrangement. Some groups require people to join formally as members but allow invited guests. Others are open to anyone and everyone on a casual 'drop in' basis.

Another form of business networking is the type whose primary objective is exchanging leads and contacts. The purpose of this kind of group is to generate referrals for its members. You get to know the other members in the group through regular meetings or one-to-one exchanges. The other members look out for opportunities for you and you do the same for them. These groups meet weekly, require committed membership and allow only one member from each profession or industry. The membership fees can be high, which is why a prerequisite is that members must attend every meeting (otherwise they can be asked to leave). These private business-referral groups operate at both national and local level. Most Chambers of Commerce operate business-referral groups. They can be an excellent way of meeting representatives from bigger businesses and can prove enormously productive and rewarding should this style of networking work for you.

We should give as we would receive, cheerfully, quickly, and without hesitation; for there is no grace in a benefit that sticks to the fingers.

Seneca, Roman philosopher, statesman and dramatist

(*c* 4 BC–AD 65)

Depending on whether you are employed by a large corporation or are a small business owner or self-employed freelancer, a number of organizations act as lobbying groups for small businesses. These can be well attended but you will probably meet lots of other small business owners. In which case don't make this your only form of networking event.

Professional associations and industry-specific groups are another form of networking. They are organized around an industry or profession and can be found for almost any occupation that exists. Depending on whether you are directed to these by your professional body, institute or association, the main objectives are to meet colleagues and competitors and to stay informed about the current state of your industry sector. If you take this route, the best way to widen your network is to ask your clients, business partners and other contacts if you can visit their professional networking groups.

There are an enormous number of not-for-profit organizations. They exist primarily to provide services at a national or local level. There are charitable, fundraising, civic, community, political and religious groups. If you wish to become involved with any of these, you are likely to meet like-minded people and have the opportunity to contribute to your community at the same time. They are extremely rewarding and well worth getting involved with if you have an amount of time you can commit.

If you have a hobby or special interest, there are lots of fun groups that exist so that enthusiasts can meet and exchange information and ideas. Whatever you enjoy doing as a leisure pursuit, there's bound to be an organization you can join. From aerobics to zoology there's bound to be a club or association that has been established for devotees. Just by getting to know people in a social setting it is possible to establish connections that lead to business relationships.

Getting to know the hierarchy and how it works

Key point
The best networks are information-rich, collaborative, high-trust environments. To be part of a vibrant network it is best to start simply.

The first thing to do when you join a networking group – whatever sort it is – is to make yourself valuable. Do your research. If you are meeting people at professional conferences, be ready to present some useful information. Even if you are a member of a small local club, offer to give a talk to other members of the group. This is not showing off, it is simply making other people aware that you are keen to keep yourself updated professionally or are socially aware and a valuable asset.

Invest some time in polishing your networking skills and work out where your existing contacts come from and where new ones might fit in. It is worth spending a bit of time categorizing them. Think about who they are, and what they are. Decision makers are people who can award business contracts, or who have the power to agree to something that you want to happen. An influencer is someone whose word carries weight if they mention you to the decision maker. (Influencers may sometimes be referred to as recommenders.) A bridge is someone who can introduce you to another person you want to make contact with, whom you might not otherwise reach. A link is a mutual connection between you and someone else and which helps establish credibility and trust with the new person. Finally, a gatekeeper is the person who stands between you and your desired contact – always be *extra* nice to them.

> *If a man does not make new acquaintance as he advances through life, he will soon find himself left alone. A man, Sir, should keep his friendships in constant repair.*
>
> Samuel Johnson (1709–1784)

If you have attended a few networking events you might have seen that the majority of people you meet are independent coaches, consultants or small business owners. If you are seeking to build a network of contacts in the corporate world, how are you to do it from there? Most of the people you probably want to meet are the employees of larger organizations. But these people have a job to do and limited time in which to do it. Networking is not high on their priority list, unless they are looking to change jobs. Large organizations have a corporate marketing department looking after the company profile, so if a member of the organization attends networking events it is most likely to be someone from the business development team looking for leads.

Many people working in large organizations don't attend networking events. However, they do attend industry conferences, seminars and training courses. They also go to awards dinners, press launches and social events. The best way to network into larger organization is to adjust your strategy and think like them. Aim to get yourself invited to the same events that these people attend. Maybe you already have some contacts who can help introduce you to someone they know in one of your target organizations. Be clear about what you want them to say about you when they make the introduction. When networking with large organizations, be prepared for the long haul. Nothing will be achieved quickly and even when you've been introduced to the right person you do need to bear your long-term strategy in mind. As long as you have clear goals in mind and are focused about what you want to achieve, you should have a much greater level of success.

Movers and shakers, winners and losers

So, who do you want to get to know? Have you made a list? Before starting out on your strategic networking campaign compile your wish list: the people you would like to know. Research who is on the way up or on the way down in your profession, industry sector, local neighbourhood or whatever area you are operating in. Depending on the reason for your networking, you should put together a detailed list of who's who and why you need to get closer to them.

So how do you go about identifying the relevant people? If you need to connect with a number of the 'great and the good' for the purpose of, say, fundraising for your chosen charity, don't risk trying to get straight to them. High-profile people have learned a few things on their way up, and one of them is to equip themselves with effective gatekeepers. You are unlikely to get past them unless you are a skilled con artist. The best way is to look out for intermediaries – people who could act as 'bridges' or 'introducers' to them. It's a lot easier to contact a person slightly beyond your reach if you hang on to the coat tails of someone who is already established in their network. This may require a degree of patience on your part but it is an important and useful piece of advice. Being introduced to a high-profile person by someone they trust is far and away the best means of getting in front of them.

Everyone, as has been mentioned before, has their own unique range of contacts. You may want to obtain increased knowledge of a certain geographical area or a certain industry sector. To source information about this, you need to look out for people who are already well networked in that relevant field. If you engage in conversations with other professionals you may obtain the names of people of influence. Keep an eye or ear on other useful sources of information such as the local and national press, TV and radio networks, professional journals, magazines and the internet.

If you do this methodically, you will in time be able to establish contact with all the people on your list. Try to vary your means of approach, for example by letter, phone call, face-to-face meeting or e-mail. As long as you ensure that the communication method is professional and to the point, you are likely to get a positive response. Should you not do so, don't take it personally. It is usually just a matter of work overload and lack of time. Don't despair, but take the opportunity the next time to introduce yourself and start the ball rolling once again.

Who goes there, and why?

It seems to me that people have vast potential. Most people can do extraordinary things if they have the confidence or take the risks. Yet most people don't. They sit in front of the TV and treat life as if it goes on forever.

Philip Adams

When you start thinking about how to implement your networking strategy, you will have to consider what types of people you're adding to your contacts, how you wish to deal with them and whether there is any particular purpose. Some people, you may find, resist overtures of friendship and are harder to build relationships with. If you are new to the process, have a look for some friendly, open characters who are fairly relaxed about meeting people and are not likely to freeze you out at first glance.

Assertive, warm characters will welcome you and be friendly. They are open-minded individuals and are quite secure and confident in themselves. They are likely to ask why you are approaching them, and once they understand who you are and what you do, will probably support you in your attempts. As long as they understand the purpose behind your networking and can see that you are professional, they will be happy to help you if there is a chance of gaining something themselves. They take a personal interest in everyone they know and are proactive individuals. If you are in their network they will want to have up-to-date knowledge about you and your work.

Accommodating, warm characters will give you a warm welcome, but this is the same response everyone will get. Their attitude will not mean that you are particularly special and they will express their feelings, which may not be entirely along the same lines as yours. These people will require more convincing than the assertive, warm characters above but you should tell them why you would like to progress the relationship. Be professional; keep your tone conversational and flexible. Position yourself as a friendly contact with a willingness to help them. They will probably prove a useful contact to have over time but are likely to have an indirect approach to helping you rather than dealing with it personally.

Accommodating, cold characters are more difficult to deal with than the others. Take the lead when connecting with them and show that you know what you are doing when you initiate the contact. They may listen quietly and it will be difficult for you to know whether they approve of your approaches or not. If they ask questions, these are likely to be concise, factual and open. If you are positive, polite yet persistent, you may not get a response immediately but they may say they are prepared to consider helping you at a later stage. Keep in touch with them because they will expect you to do so.

Assertive, cold characters are the most difficult to approach and do not like networking. They are not open-minded where business relationships are concerned. Their negative attitude is not personal; they use it as a shield. Small talk should be kept to an absolute minimum. The best way to make any headway with these people is to enlist help from someone who is already known to them, and use them as a persuader or facilitator, to help you make progress with them.

> *It is absurd to divide people into good and bad. People are either charming or tedious.*
>
> Oscar Wilde (1854–1900)

Networking can be a huge challenge if you lack confidence. If going it alone seems too tough at the outset, perhaps teaming up with a colleague or associate would give vital moral support. You can introduce them to other people, and praise their business or virtues while making the introduction. This is something you can do a lot more easily for someone else than for yourself. And it is twice as effective when done on behalf of someone else. They in turn do the same for you. The bonus to this method is that you can double your efforts and contacts because you can share your connections with your colleague.

Actions speak louder than words

Here are a few tips on behaviour and etiquette when networking.

Before you attend an event do your homework. Make sure you know why you're going. How important is it? What persuaded you to accept the invitation? Have you got a particular agenda? If you don't understand why you are attending, you won't make the best use of the opportunities it presents. If you're particularly nervous, can you go with a colleague or a friend?

Depending on the formality of the occasion, you may get to see the guest list beforehand. Prepare yourself for whom you might encounter. If you have time to do so, create a target list of potential prospects. Should you be able to identify a friendly face or two by scanning through the names, you will at least have one or two identified contacts. If you don't recognize anyone you know and it is a step into the complete unknown, check the dress code.

Appearances can make or break an encounter. It's better to be over-dressed than too casual. Arriving in ripped jeans (even if they do have a designer label) or scruffy sports clothes is okay for some occasions but it won't add to your confidence if everyone except you is smartly dressed.

Correct location? Some venues look or sound much like another and you can waste hours searching for them. Make sure you are in the right place. It sounds elementary, I know. But some conference suites in hotels have similar-sounding names, some restaurants are called the same. It is possible to be in the wrong place, even if you arrive at the right time. Reaching a venue when the bar has run dry, the doors are closing and they're putting out the garbage sacks is rather dispiriting. Everyone messes up sometime or other, but it's certainly not helpful when you're new to networking.

Try to be positive and outwardly confident. It will make you stand out above others. Don't worry if you have butterflies; research shows that over 90 per cent of people feel fear about walking into a room full of strangers.

4

Networking in the virtual community

When I took office, only high-energy physicists had ever heard of what is called the worldwide web... Now even my cat has its own page.

Bill Clinton

Whether you like it or use it regularly, the internet is an excellent invention. It's something that can be used effectively for virtual networking. The internet has many benefits, not least its ease of use – and it's available 24/7/365. You could say it sits there just begging to be taken advantage of. If you're not particularly computer literate you might be hesitant about using it. For those lacking experience or confidence, real networking is a challenge. Add to that anxiety the prospect of dealing with the entire online world, and you could be forgiven if you're reaching for the panic button. You might feel that it's rather like stepping off a precipice, in the dark, into the unknown. The regular bursts of publicity about identity theft, fraud and various other cyber crimes only increase the unease in those of a nervous disposition. These stories add to people's phobias, real or imagined, and drive some to a decision to keep the virtual world at arm's length.

However, should you be a shy person, one who finds face-to-face dealings with other people scary, if you're the type who embarrasses easily and have a tendency to feel inferior whenever you are in a group situation, perhaps networking in the virtual community is the opportunity you've been waiting for. Physical networking that involves walking into a room full of strangers has been known to reduce grown men to tears. Remove that obstacle and it might encourage you to take up online networking with enthusiasm and glee. It doesn't matter what the weather's like; you don't have to travel far; or get dressed up in smart clothes; or spend money buying tickets to events. It's so easy to do – anytime, anywhere. All you need is a computer, access to the internet and, as I explain later, a personal e-mail address. What are you waiting for? Why not give it some serious consideration? You will find there are commonalities running throughout this book which relate to important points mentioned in this chapter. What you have read up to now (and hopefully will continue to read) is relevant and applicable in many instances. Above all, you will get better results from your online networking if you possess the four key attributes, which I'll repeat once again, in case you've forgotten them: curiosity (like asking questions); generosity (the ability to give and not just take); confidence (you are trustworthy and honest); and motivation (you have a purpose and you stick to it).

The development of the internet has been so successful and rapid that it now impacts on everyone's life in many ways. Areas that were under an individual's control are now subject to the vast, intangible yet omnipresent medium of cyberspace. These so-called 'enhancements' that the worldwide web has given everyone are still subject to much debate. There are valid arguments and opinions from either side. Is the internet a positive or negative influence? What should or should not be done about it?

Key point

The plain fact is that the internet is here to stay. It has given rise to some corrupt practices, which is regrettable. On the other hand it provides overwhelming benefits to millions: constantly accessible knowledge and easy communication with the entire world. The internet is a staggeringly powerful force that dramatically impacts on everyone's life.

The role of the internet in networking

The internet is like alcohol in some sense. It accentuates what you would do anyway. If you want to be a loner, you can be more alone. If you want to connect, it makes it easier to connect.
Esther Dyson (interview in *Time* magazine, October 2005)

It would be easy enough at this stage to lose focus and become completely distracted. Much time could be spent discussing the use of the internet in general, and its effect on society in particular. This chapter is specifically about the role of the internet with respect to networking; how it works, what you can do and whether or not it is safe. This is what will be discussed here. For reference and to put things in context, the internet is a network of interconnected computers whose origins date back to the 1960s in the US military. The commercialization of the internet did not take place until the 1990s. Its development has been so rapid that, at the time of writing, approximately one quarter of the planet now has access to it. Compared with other statistics, the fact that internet access is currently available to 25 per cent of the world's population after such a short time is amazing. The percentage that has access to sanitized drinking water, for example, is roughly the same. In contrast, just think how long ago irrigation methods were invented and how slow the progress in this area has been.

Key point

The purpose of the internet is to share information. It could be argued that the concept of physical networking is exactly the same. In this case, the internet is nothing more than a huge virtual reality that can be harnessed by the willing individual for the sole objective of networking.

Being the cunning beast that it is, the internet has now evolved to such an extent that it has many different ways of allowing the avid networker to network. In fact, as you will see, you are literally spoiled for choice (http://en.wikipedia.org/wiki/internet).

Online networking – the various media

On the internet, nobody knows you're a dog.
Peter Steiner (cartoon in *New Yorker* magazine, 5 July 1993)

The development of the internet has allowed a host of different networking media to develop. Outlined below are the main types that you are likely to encounter. Depending on how you want to network in the virtual world, or what you want to network about, this would drive your decision on which method to use. Each has different pros and cons. As a general rule, the greater the variety of methods you use, the more successful your networking will be. You can use as many of them as you want – or all of them.

E-mail

In its crudest form, networking via the internet was made possible by the establishment of electronic mail (e-mail as it is known now) in tandem with the method of exchanging digital messages.

Provided someone has an e-mail address you can communicate electronically with them. This means that interpersonal human-to-human contact is feasible via the internet. The first e-mail message was allegedly sent early in the 1970s. However, it was not until the internet boom that its use became so widespread. The benefits of e-mail are obvious: it is quick, free and easy (provided you know how to work a computer).

Key point

E-mail offers huge benefits for both businesses and individuals. It has become the most widely used method of distributing important information, from single person-to-person exchanges to widespread distribution lists consisting of tens of thousands of e-mail addresses.

For example, at the press of a button, in seconds a multinational corporation can inform its entire global workforce that there has been a change of chairman.

E-mail has some problems, in terms of communication logistics. You cannot guarantee that people will actually read the e-mail even if it arrives safely in their inbox. With some applications the sender can request (but it is not a requirement) that the recipient sends an automatic message when the e-mail arrives, to confirm delivery. This won't, however, ensure that it's read or acted upon. If you don't have someone's correct e-mail address in your database, they won't receive the message at all. E-mail has a big advantage in that you can send attachments with your message (provided the file isn't too large); a document or photograph is the most usual. Getting an e-mail address is the first step into the world of virtual networking. If you don't have one and you'd like to do some online networking, your internet service provider (ISP) should supply one for you. If the ISP hasn't provided one, then visit Hotmail, Yahoo or Google Mail – there are many other mail services too – and set yourself up with a free e-mail account today. Should you want to use it for business purposes, you can embed a 'signature' into your e-mail. This can state your job title, contact details, company name and strap line, logo etc. In effect this can act as your virtual business card. (See Chapter 5 for more information on business cards and their use.) (http://en.wikipedia.org/wiki/E-mail)

Instant messaging

Another popular form of online communication is IMS (instant messaging service) or SMS (short messaging service). This requires the person you wish to communicate with to be signed up to the same messaging service, which makes it slightly different to e-mail. When this is the case (and it does require you to have some friends already) you can have a 'real time' conversation with them by simply typing lines of chat in a box.

Key point

The instantaneousness of instant messaging and its negligible cost – you could be talking to a relative on the other side of the world – make far more economic sense than a phone call.

Instant messaging can be quite revealing too – you will discover whether or not your correspondent can spell, since there's no time to run a spell check. There are many instant messaging services to choose from: MSN, AIM and Google Mail, to name just three. Google Mail, for example, has an application within it that allows you to chat with any other Google Mail contacts you have, rather than e-mail them. This is a quick and useful way of contacting people instantly – you can see if they are online and available. If they are, you can chat to them right away. Although more associated with social and private use, some corporations have introduced internal instant messaging systems. The idea behind this is to drive efficiency and improve communication on an inter-departmental basis. It certainly makes internal networking easier, should you be thinking of doing this. Don't worry if you have a disagreement with a colleague or someone starts plaguing you with messages or you end up involved in heated discussions with colleagues who are less busy than you and for whom you don't have time; a block option is available that prevents others from messaging you. It doesn't tell them you've done this. To them it simply looks like you're not online.

Chat rooms

These are a variant on the instant messenger theme. The best description possibly is that they are effectively an online conference facility. This virtual networking is really versatile, isn't it? The chat room is affiliated to a certain subject – take for example, the popular TV show *Lost*. Its chat room provides individuals who are interested in the programme the opportunity to discuss theories, critique episodes and generally debate the show with other interested parties. Obviously the scope of what different chat rooms do varies; they are not all deeply rooted in pop culture. For instance, software developers might join a chat room to discuss the benefits and issues of a beta version of a new Windows programme just being released by Microsoft for trial.

Chat rooms generally have rules of behaviour to ensure that no one misbehaves. Depending on the degree of strictness of the moderator, participants of a chat room might be banned from further activity if, due to a difference of opinion, they insult other members. In addition, the chat room provides an online area where like-minded individuals can congregate and discuss common interests. If you are checking the similarities with physical networking, this is how to make new contacts and establish mutual interests. This is how many successful friendships are formed.

Forums

A forum is another type of discussion room for those with shared interests. It is normally attached to the internet site of a particular subject. For instance, most pop bands have a forum on their website. This is where fans can discuss songs, upcoming tours and forthcoming albums. They could even debate which member of the band was most likely to have voted UKIP in the European elections. Again, it does not have to be associated with pop culture. Internet sites on all subjects can have forums.

Key point

The distinction between a forum and a chat room is that forums are generally more organized and have specific topic threads. The chat room is much more as it sounds, informal with lots of random chatter on many topics.

Annoyingly for those of an impatient disposition, forums do not function in real time. You post a reply and it may be minutes, hours or days before it is responded to; sometimes it never is. Some forum members have a profile with an avatar (an irritating image with which an individual chooses to represent themselves virtually; this 'logo' appears on every post they write). There is also the facility to PM (private message) other forum members should you wish to do so. In simple terms, this means the ability to respond personally to another member of the forum without it being visible to the rest of the members (or the browsing public). Browsing forums and topic threads as a guest is possible. However, posting comments requires membership status, so you'll have to join up.

Social networking sites

Social networking sites are the Big One. In terms of online networking this is the sector that has recently seen the most rapid and biggest growth and use. The number of people who use it, and the amount of time they now spend online, are phenomenal. Social networking sites are being used every minute of every day all over the world, by millions of people. A few years ago it was all about a site called MySpace. The most popular one now is Facebook. Depending on geographical location this can vary, however. For instance, in Asia, Friendster has a far larger market share than it does in the West. The site called Twitter is now beginning to infringe upon Facebook's dominance. (But Twitter has significant differences – so more about it later.)

Key point

A social networking site is basically about creating online communities of people. These people share interests and activities and allow others to view the information they provide and interact with the community.

Most communities share common features, but each has their own unique slant or take on the general social networking site framework. The framework is an application where you are able to create a profile for yourself, upload pictures or video – pretty much anything. On your profile you can list your interests, likes and dislikes – again almost anything you want. This framework allows you to become 'friends' with other users. You can become 'friends' either because you know them in reality already, or because you like their online profile. If you have a passion for origami, scrambled eggs and the films of Ingmar Bergman from 1955 to 1965 you can find others who share those interests and become instant, virtual friends. Most social networking sites have their own in-house version of e-mail or instant messaging service, which allows you to contact other members through the site. Obviously it is only member-to-member communication that is available through the site.

Are you keeping up at the back? Now, social networking sites can be divided into two different categories: internal social networking (ISN) or external social networking (ESN). ISN is a close/private community that consists of a group of people within a company, association, really any type of membership organization that you would either pay or be eligible to join by virtue of your profession or qualifications. The only other way of joining one would be to receive an invitation to join from an existing member. Somewhat confusingly, it is possible to create ISNs within some ESNs. Facebook works like this. You might feel obligated to set up a sub-group to mourn the loss of Michael Jackson, which anyone who uses Facebook can subscribe to and which you could invite people to join (since you'd know they share your passion for the late King of Pop).

Key point

ESNs are basically open to all web users to join. However, they are likely to be based around a particular theme, or have a purpose behind instigating the type of virtual networking.

Do you remember Friends Reunited? This was set up so that former school friends would have a chance to track each other down and find other former classmates they had lost touch with. Match.com is an online dating site that gives singles the chance to meet other singles virtually before (perhaps) arranging a date. There's something for everyone and there's probably a social networking site for almost anything you can think of. If not, why not start one? Sites also cover medical issues, such as weight loss or pregnancy, special interests and, of course, business needs.

External social networking sites have some restrictions. They cannot accept people just randomly joining up. Any friend requests have to be approved by the person being requested, to allow the requester to be added. The requester, having been given permission to join, can then have access to view other members' profiles and create their own. There are obviously some privacy controls; these allow you to decide how much information about yourself you wish to have displayed, and you can also limit your friends' access to this.

Personal social networking sites

It would be impossible here to list all the personal networking sites – there are far too many. If you are really interested, there's plenty of information to be found on the internet. Just Google 'social networking sites'. For the purposes of keeping this chapter a reasonable length, only the two most significant, MySpace and Facebook, are discussed here.

The first social networking site really to explode on to the cultural consciousness was MySpace. It was created in 2003 and grew rapidly, becoming the biggest social networking site on the web by 2006. It now has approximately 190 million members. MySpace came into its own with its MySpace music feature. This allows pop bands to create their own portal for fan interaction. This has resulted in many bands launching successful careers – the Arctic Monkeys probably being the best known example. Recognizing the dominance and importance of the internet in the world of media, Rupert Murdoch's News Corporation bought MySpace for the relatively small sum of $580 million in July 2005.

The restless world of the internet being what it is, with its relentless progress, it was not long before Facebook appeared. This has produced a real threat to MySpace's social networking dominance. It was initially invented as a networking tool exclusively for Harvard University students in 2004. Not surprisingly it developed and grew, opening in September 2006 with access for anyone with a valid e-mail address and who was over the age of 13. Since then it has grown phenomenally, with current membership standing at just over 150 million. This statistic shows the speed at which you can 'meet' new people by using the internet. To meet over 150 million people physically you'd need to start networking very early on in life, perhaps in your pram or in the womb. Facebook is actually the most used social networking site on the internet, having overtaken MySpace at the beginning of 2009.

Discussing the distinctions between these two leviathans isn't easy since they have many common features. However, MySpace allows users to customize their profile, while Facebook just has a standard template. Facebook is built around affiliated networks. For example, say you live in Brighton in England and attended Aberdeen University in Scotland, it would be sensible to join the Facebook's Brighton and Hove network as well as the Aberdeen University one. You might get a job at Tesco's, and then you could join the Tesco network.

Key point

Facebook's affiliated network approach gives you the opportunity to find people you might already know, or get into contact with people who are likely to have more mutual connections with you, and vice versa.

MySpace doesn't really work like this. It is somewhat notorious for users receiving lots of spam requests from groups or individuals – and you have absolutely no idea who they are. Don't be put off here: this could be a positive aspect of online networking if this is something you would relish. You are constantly being exposed to potentially new and exciting people and experiences, but it can also be quite annoying. Interestingly, recently there have been various social studies on the phenomenon of online social networking. It appears there are clear class distinctions in society as to which site you are most likely to use. Now, what a surprise.

Business social networking sites and applications

Due to the rapid rise of online social networking sites and their popularity, businesses were keen to exploit this new phenomenon in a variety of ways. Initially this explosion had fundamentally shaken the foundations of the world of business and work.

Key point

If you are a small business or entrepreneur, this is as amazing as it is exciting. Potentially you can contact and expand your customer base extremely easily, with no increase to your overheads.

First, social networks connect people at low cost and they are also an excellent customer service tool as clients and consumers have a means of directly contacting their service provider. This can only improve, enhance and strengthen customer relationships and client and consumer satisfaction.

Social networking sites also provide businesses with an opportunity to brand and promote themselves, as well as conduct market research by interacting virtually with their clientele. For example, if Coca-Cola planned to launch a new variety of Coke, they could create a Facebook group about it. This would allow any potentially interested consumers to have the chance to find out more about it, and simultaneously spread the word about its launch.

Social networking sites can also be used for recruiting staff and to learn about new technologies and competitors. In addition, they can drive traffic to their own online sites, while encouraging their consumers and clients to have discussions on how to improve or change products or services.

On social networking sites, people's profiles contain valuable data about their likes, dislikes, hobbies, lifestyle and interests.

This is information a corporate marketing department would die for, to help them work out how to launch a new product. If you are familiar with Facebook, you might notice that, similarly to Google, ads are displayed down the right-hand side of the page. These are products or services that cyberspace deems you might be interested in. If you click on these adverts, you generate revenue for Facebook. The wealth of data that social networking sites have accrued about their users is a hugely valuable commodity. Indeed, it is so important it forms part of the debate over the privacy of internet users. Just consider how much information Google has about everyone who uses its search engine. It's almost impossible to imagine. But no doubt you are all upstanding citizens with impeccable credentials and spotless backgrounds. You have nothing to hide, so all this should be of no consequence.

Apart from the potential benefits for businesses from everyone who uses social networking sites, there are also business networking sites. These include the obvious ones such as recruitment sites, which list career and work opportunities. Sites like peopleperhour.com are where businesses post work that they need done, then people get to bid for it. Outsourcing work to an online workforce is a great method of reducing costs.

There are also examples of social networking sites being used for business purposes, such as LinkedIn.com. This site aims to connect professionals. It has been very successful since its launch in 2003 and has become the current Facebook of the business world, with over 40 million users in over 200 countries.

Key point

Registered users are able to use LinkedIn.com to maintain a list of contacts that they know and trust in business. Trusted contacts are listed as their 'connections' and a registered user is then able to invite anyone to become a connection.

The idea behind this is that the list of connections can then be put to a variety of uses. This could be from straightforward networking by browsing lists of connections, to locating jobs and business opportunities (since these can be recommended to you by your connections). Employers can advertise jobs and carry out research on potential candidates. Of course, you can research potential employers and find out if you have an 'in' at their organizations. The closed membership of LinkedIn.com means that an existing member needs to invite you to join. This helps to build trust and confidence in the network and gives some protection so that people with dubious motives cannot get access to this virtual world.

(http://en.wikipedia.org/wiki/Social_networking), (http://en.wikipedia.org/wiki/Myspace), (http://en.wikipedia.org/wiki/Facebook), (http://www.pcworld.com/article/134633-8/facebook_and_myspace_whats_the_difference.html), (http://www.selfgrowth.com/socialnetworkingwebsites.html)

Twitter

Previously I mentioned Twitter only in passing but it is in fact important enough to have its own section. Now you've read this far, hopefully you will understand the reason for this. Interestingly, Twitter does not fit the mould of anything discussed so far. It is unusual. Like most internet applications, it shares common features with other online social networking sites. However, it just happens to have caught society's imagination: Twitter is a micro-blogging service. While a blog is an internet page in which you write about whatever you want, in as many words as you want, micro-blogging is where you are able to post micro-blogs of up to 140 characters each time. This is similar to the status updates you can make on Facebook. Generally the blogs are about what you are doing, but they could cover any subject.

To sign up on Twitter you will need an e-mail address. Once you've done this, you can begin tweeting to your heart's content.

These mini-blogs are called 'tweets'. (Isn't that lovely?) Of course you will need to create a profile for yourself.

> **Key point**
>
> Using Twitter, you can see what other people are doing by opting to 'follow' their updates. Anyone who wants to know what you are tweeting on about will have to become one of your 'followers'. The tweets are listed in chronological order on your Twitter homepage from all the people you follow.

When explained like this, it seems fairly straightforward (which it is), but somewhat bizarrely it has become a huge social phenomenon. Part of its attraction in this celebrity-obsessed age is the fact that it allows you to follow all the celebrity icons everyone is so fascinated with. So, should you wish to know what Stephen Fry had for his breakfast this morning, now you can find out.

There is a bit of etiquette where Twitter is concerned, and there are a few things to remember in order to get the most out of the application. Don't tweet too frequently, as this could just end up annoying your followers. They might even abandon you, heaven forbid. If you wish to respond directly to a tweet that someone has made, you simply add @ before their twitter name to ensure it appears in their 'replies' section, rather than getting lost in the stream of tweets on their homepage. You can 're-tweet', which means posting someone else's tweet to your followers. If you want to do this, type RT before you re-tweet. It is also possible to filter tweets so that if, say, you are tweeting about a particular subject – the recent Iranian election, for example – then you would hash-tag your tweet *#iranianelection* and then tweet. If you were searching for tweets about the Iranian election, all you have to do is type *#iranianelection* into the search field and it would display them all.

Once you get your head round it, Twitter is an excellent tool for interaction. You can have conversations, ask questions, network and find out information very quickly. It is worth spending some time fiddling about to familiarize yourself with it, so that you can make the application work for you. In terms of business, it is useful as it can ensure that vital information is dissipated through the business community very quickly. For example, you could be a software developer working on a new web application, and another software developer working in California discovers a fresh virus that your software needs to be secured from. If this Californian developer tweets about their discovery, you can then find out about it quickly and make the necessary adjustments to your piece of software. In an instant, your new product is protected from this virus. How much better than discovering the problem months down the line, after a lot more expensive development work has been done. (http://news.bbc.co.uk/1/hi/programmes/click_online/8017373.stm)

What are the risks?

It shouldn't be too much of a surprise that the internet has evolved into a force strong enough to reflect the greatest hopes and fears of those who use it. After all, it was designed to withstand nuclear war, not just the puny huffs and puffs of politicians and religious fanatics.

Denise Caruso (digital commerce columnist, *New York Times*)

Having outlined various ways in which it is possible to network online, what actually are the risks involved in this? Is there potential for misuse and abuse? The media are full of horror stories about various abuses that have happened on Facebook or MySpace. These can range from people pretending to be other people, or people lying in profiles and the like. In terms of pitfalls there are three main problem areas: privacy, transparency and accountability.

Privacy

Privacy is a problem because by doing any networking online you are providing a lot of information about yourself. Data theft can be an issue, as the information that you have provided might be useful to a dubious third party wanting to engage in illegal activity. For example, if enough of your details are obtainable, it might be possible to submit a credit card application in your name. The TV presenter and celebrity Jeremy Clarkson famously published his bank details in his Sunday newspaper column claiming that all the scare-mongering about data theft was overblown. Unfortunately for him, a member of the public used this information to set up a direct debit in favour of a charity, paid out of Mr Clarkson's bank account.

Key point

The obvious lesson from this is not to put any sensitive personal information online.

There are further issues surrounding data. For example, it is claimed that Facebook and other social networking sites retain your information even after your account with them has been deactivated. It is also claimed that internet companies keep records of e-mails that have been sent and that Google stores your search history for the last six months.

There are further human consequences in terms of social networking. The use of the Friends Reunited site, to name just one, where school friends could reacquaint themselves with former classmates, was responsible for the breakdown of many otherwise seemingly successful personal relationships. Old flames were able to rekindle romances that had long been forgotten, and unrequited lovers suddenly had the opportunity for a bit of 'requiting'. With hindsight, it created a number of unforeseen and unhappy consequences for some families. Suddenly what had seemed satisfying because other things were unobtainable had changed. The satisfactory was not good enough; there had to be more and better opportunities. The saddest aspect was the innocent victims: children who had had secure family units witnessing their parents splitting up and forming other relationships.

Key point

There's a huge potential risk here – the effect of the virtual world (it's not real but you'd like some if you could get it) impacting on the real world (what you've got but is it worth anything?).

Some people are now actually creating 'virtual lives' and living in both real and virtual worlds.

Going back to sites like Facebook, for example, say your boss wants to add you as a friend. Now to deny a friend request from your boss could lead to some serious disharmony in the work place, so to avoid this you accept. But now your boss has access to a whole host of your personal information. It's the sort of information that perhaps you'd rather not have shared, and vice versa. Maybe you didn't want to know that your boss attended a wild party this weekend – let alone see the pictures – too much information. Then there are the all-too-familiar stories of people taking a 'sickie' and on the same day photos of them appearing on Facebook and looking... er... not all that ill. Then your boss finds out, which (in one particular instance already) has led to a dismissal.

Obviously, with things like Twitter there is the problem that once you tweet you cannot 'untweet'. Thus if you wish to post potentially offensive opinions or comments, remember it will be there for *anyone* to be able to see. If you want to support the BNP, that's great – but other people might not be so keen on hearing about it.

> **Key point**
>
> Of course, there is also the old, classic problem of your sending an e-mail to the unintended recipient or accidentally hitting the 'Reply All' button, which sends the message to all the addresses that the original communication was sent to.

Remember, it is the world wide web – so information can, in an instant, go *everywhere*.

Transparency

Transparency is the term that relates, in a virtual world, to the degree of clarity within interactions. As you are not actually face to face with anyone, it isn't real – everything is done via computer. In other chapters in this book, much is made of the importance of eye contact and feeling the physical vibes of other people. But in the virtual world you really don't have any way of verifying what or who you are interacting with. In essence this is what transparency claims to be.

> **Key point**
>
> Transparency issues arise with any online networking you do, because you can't tell who you are networking with – they could be anybody doing anything. You certainly don't know what they are doing with the information you are providing to them.

Take the sickening example of how often sexual predators use the tactic online of setting up fake profiles on networking sites. They do this in order to interact with children, and their intention is to achieve far worse. In terms of online dating, similar problems can occur. How do you know that the picture you see of the prospective online date is actually them? Are they really a billionaire with a château in France, a Learjet and a mansion in Belgravia, London? Does the company you are hoping to do business with really have a net profit last year of US$1.4 million? Google's motto might well be 'Do no evil', but what are they *really* intending to do with all the information they have accrued about your online habits?

This is not intended to panic or scare anyone away from internet networking, but it is meant as a reality check on the virtual world. Take it, if you like, more as a warning that all might not be what it seems. Beware, and take care – just as you would if you were walking down the street and wanted to cross the road, or driving your car on a busy motorway in the rush hour. Taking sensible precautions when dealing with the virtual world is simple good advice – take heed and apply the same caution as you do in the real world.

Accountability

This is the third problem for any internet use and, by association of course, networking. Considering the huge amount of things that can happen regarding the internet, there are seriously low levels of accountability. The internet in a lot of ways is highly unregulated, causing some commentators to liken it to the Wild West in its heyday. The Wild West at one time was so uncontrolled that people had free rein and could pretty much do what they wanted. There was no recourse to any laws because they did not exit.

Key point

When you consider the internet, the best example of lack of accountability is file sharing. Yes, this is illegal, but in terms of, say, the music industry, there is such a lack of agreement on how to tackle this problem that the likelihood of any solution seems remote.

This is primarily due to the large number of offenders, and the large number of interested parties within the music industry. These range from label employees, the artists, distributors and shops. Because of this situation, any sort of compensation would have to be spilt so many ways that it makes the resolution extremely complicated. Add to this the problem of there being so many internet service providers, all of whom may have a different perspective on this. These companies are unwilling to provide the details of alleged file sharers to prosecutors as it is not a requirement of the law. To complicate matters still further, this is a global issue; but there is no world government to lay down the law for every country to follow. As you can see, it becomes impossible to regulate. If you were file sharing in the USA on an American site you would be put in prison for it; yet if you were doing this in the USA on an Australian site, where it is not illegal, you might not have broken the law.

Again in terms of social networking, take this as a warning that the unregulated nature of the internet can be exploited. However, at the same time, this should also be seen as an inspirational message. Almost anything can be achieved online – you simply need the idea and the motivation to do it. Just like networking in the physical world, with a little curiosity, confidence and motivation anything is possible. So networking online is surely an excellent starting place for those who want to meet millions of virtual friends.

(http://www.guardian.co.uk/commentisfree/2007/apr/25/
thedarksideoffacebook), (http://news.bbc.co.uk/1/hi/programmes/
click_online/8017373.stm), (http://en.wikipedia.org/wiki/Social_
networking), (http://news.bbc.co.uk/1/hi/entertainment/
7174760.stm), (http://www.guardian.co.uk/media/pda/2007/
nov/20/facebookthefinelinebetween)

Safeguards that can be applied

The main safeguard you can apply in all of this is something
everyone possesses (though some are more generously endowed
than others): common sense. If you are not familiar with, or comfortable using, the internet, take steps to improve your knowledge
and skill as soon as possible. This would help you to feel more
comfortable. Google and Wikipedia are both excellent learning
resources and an easy means of retrieving massive amounts of
information on subjects you know nothing about. *Use them.*

Key point
It should go without saying: make sure your computer has the
necessary firewall, antivirus and spyware software installed and
do make it a rule that you regularly back up data and download
available upgrades. Other than that, common sense is your best
means of defence from anything bad happening.

If you find yourself on a website that says you have won a million
pounds and to claim the money all you have to do is 'click here'
– *don't.* Why? Because you haven't. You wouldn't buy a diamond
necklace, which you're told is actually worth £100,000, for £200
from that bloke in the pub who needs to shift it fast, would you?
Think of the phoney million-pound prize as the virtual equivalent
of the dodgy geezer with the swag in your local boozer. If you

receive an e-mail from an unknown source, normally a gentleman located somewhere in Africa or Indonesia asking for your bank details, don't send them to him. Delete the e-mail at once. Also, don't put your mobile number on any profiles you set up. Only give it out to real people you know, like and trust. If you fail to take these simple precautions, who knows how many oddballs might start calling you at 4 am. As mentioned earlier, the virtual experience is fun, exciting and rewarding. It is also an everyday part of life in the 21st century. Use it, take advantage of it, but you have been warned: treat it with the same amount of respect and caution as if it were an untamed animal. You don't want to get bitten.

Why you cannot afford to miss out

We've heard that a million monkeys at a million keyboards could produce the complete works of Shakespeare; now, thanks to the internet, we know that is not true.
Robert Wilensky (speech at a 1996 conference)

The reason why you cannot afford to miss out is because the internet is the present and the future. It is fast becoming the chosen medium for networking. It has already changed everyone's life and will continue to do so. If you tried, and failed, to make contact with someone recently, the answer might have come back, 'Sorry, my internet connection is down. I haven't been able to do anything all day.' Social commentators are already highlighting ways in which Twitter is changing business practices and the way people live. It is just one example of various internet applications that have created new ways to communicate, market products and services and retrieve information instantly.

Key point

The development of mobile internet technology such as the iPhone, Smartphones and WiFi allows you to access the internet on the move. Its application is no longer just for when you are at home or at the office, but all day long, anywhere. This actually increases your dependence on it and on its functionality.

It is arguable that the rise of Twitter could probably be attributed to the growth of mobile internet devices. It means that people can tweet as and when they want, wherever they may be, as they are always attached to the information highway.

There are several examples as illustrations. First, plenty of individuals use the power of the internet to get themselves jobs. One of my friends is a web designer. He went about getting a job for himself by using the internet as he hadn't the time to go through recruitment consultants and attend interviews. He'd become unfulfilled working for his previous company, so he decided to seize the initiative. He created an internet page for himself to act as a portfolio for his work. He started a blog about his work and started using Twitter to tweet about what he was doing. This basically gave him an online presence and a channel to communicate with other web designers and design companies. It just so happened that one particular design company liked his work enough to offer him a job. So my friend successfully harnessed the internet to get himself a better job by using the various applications that were on offer to him. This illustrates that it can work – and that there are physical benefits to be gained from having a virtual presence.

The second example shows how Twitter is increasingly being used as a means of communication and transfer of information, or more importantly, current affairs. Think of any headline-grabbing story – from the Mumbai terrorist attacks in 2008, to the Iranian Election results 2009, to the death of Michael Jackson in June 2009. People flocked to Twitter or other online applications to get updates or find out information about these subjects, from the constantly updated stream of information. The Michael Jackson event is credited with actually causing some areas of the internet to crash or slow down because the volume of traffic was so great. The point here is that Twitter, a micro-blogging service, is being used as a means of obtaining breaking news on current affairs. If you are not online, you could miss out on all this. The way people act has been changed dramatically by the internet. Instead of turning on the radio or TV to listen to the headlines, it's now more common to log onto the internet or go to a social networking site to get the latest news.

Key point

The phenomenal growth of the use of the internet in terms of networking is causing a merging of the previous separate components of your life. The personal and business areas are no longer divided but are being mixed together by virtue of the internet to create something else entirely.

You need to be aware of this blending of the internal and external and not react against it but go with it. Change is inevitable and is all around you. As a direct result of the internet the world has shrunk – working online transcends traditional geographical boundaries and time zones. It also merges cultures, customs and languages. Should you still be in denial in terms of the internet, you are being unrealistic. Resistance is pointless. You will not achieve anything, as it will simply carry you along, it is so strong. Best advice is to get over it, get on with it and embrace the change.

Forthcoming applications like Google Wave, which intend to combine all the social networking applications you can have into one easy-to-use platform, will, seemingly, continue this process. It may seem strange or abnormal to try and alter your perception this way. To use the old adage of sociologist Emile Durkheim, deviance or abnormal behaviour allows social change to occur by pushing the boundaries of what is considered normal practice in society. This is exactly what the internet is doing. It is a new medium by which human interaction can occur; as it develops it impacts on society. But then society has never stood still and always will change. The challenge is to ensure that the power of the internet can be harnessed not as a source of exploitation or evil but as a force for positive development, for yourself and others. Isn't that an exciting thought? (http://www.time.com/time/specials/packages/article/ 0,28804,1901188_1901207,00.html), (http://www.nytimes.com/ 2009/05/21/fashion/21whiz.html?_r=2&em=&adxnnl= 1&adxnnlx=1245237697-wVM6P1q58y0oW720yDgTuw), (http://www.time.com/time/world/article/0,8599,1905125, 00.html)

5

Business cards

*Doing business without advertising is like winking at a girl in the
dark. You know what you are doing, but nobody else does.*
Stuart Henderson Britt

Do business cards really work? Are they an aid to networking? Are
they necessary? Do they matter and how can they be used most
effectively? Business cards are a necessity for everyone in business
and for every company. They are a flexible and inexpensive way to
introduce yourself to someone new. Theirs is an essential role –
easy and convenient contact cards. When networking, the correct
use of a business card is paramount. If you don't know what to do,
you will miss potential opportunities. Even if you manage your
contacts database through your PDA and you 'beam' your contact
information to others, business cards still matter. In terms of networking in the virtual community, the role of business cards and
their use online are important. Anything you can do physically
can, it seems, be done virtually these days. So, as I have explained
in the preceding chapter, general advice on printed business cards
that you hand out to people you meet in person is equally applicable to electronic versions that you use as embedded signatures in
business communications.

In tough economic times, you cannot afford to miss any
opportunity to network successfully and bring in new business

contacts. Making new friends when markets are shrinking is the intelligent thing to do, and successful professionals look for chances where others see only closing doors. Prestigious business cards convey a lasting impression. Is it appropriate to think about revamping your calling card? Investing some time and money in designing and printing some new cards could be a shrewd move. You could begin planting seeds of potentially valuable friendships while waiting for the green shoots of recovery.

Key point

The purpose of a business card is to proffer your contact details easily to someone you meet, and at the same time enable you to ask for one of their cards in return.

Business cards can be much more than an information exchange, but this depends on the type of card you use. A quality card conveys to your new contact your corporate identity. In the same way as good personal presentation is essential if you are to create a positive and lasting first impression with someone, your business card should be written proof that underlines this. A professional business card serves as a reminder to your new business contact of who you are and what your business stands for. Business cards should be at the core of any company's marketing material and anyone who wishes to network effectively should carry them. The purpose of the business card is to capture attention, convey information and reflect the corporate identity. The person distributing the card has much the same physical responsibility in the networking arena.

Key point

It doesn't matter what business you are in or what you are trying to convey, a quality card is the ideal complement to your personal networking skills. It emphasizes that you are a professional and leaves a tangible reminder of that impression.

Anyone who is serious about networking will not leave their home or workplace without a supply of cards. As part of your networking checklist, your supply of business cards is an essential item in your toolkit. A good business card holder keeps cards in pristine condition, so it's well worth acquiring one. If you wish to come across in the best possible way, don't risk your cards letting you down by offering one that is scruffy or creased. Business cards are an important instrument when connecting with other people – and making that connection stick. It's important to have the right kind of card because it represents you as well as your company. Some people have business cards printed twice or three times a year, to keep current and ring the changes. Some businesses are more sensitive to market and economic forces, so updating your card may be required on a regular basis just to keep your details and your image fresh. In terms of networking, this helps to keep you ahead of your competitors, particularly those who do not do this. The way to maximize the use of your business cards is to design and print them in such a way that your target clients can't ignore the information on them. If you get top-quality cards, work on distributing them, then let them do the work for you. Every opportunity you have of giving a card to a new contact is a chance for you to increase your network.

The role of the business card today

Business today consists in persuading crowds.

Gerald Stanley Lee

As already described, a business card is an essential adjunct to your networking strategy. It provides easy and convenient access to your contact information and at best it should persuade people to do business with you rather than your competitors. It creates awareness among people with whom you are networking about the existence of your business and services. In short, it represents your work, your style and business sense through design and the information it provides. It can win you business and provide you with opportunities to create a vibrant network of contacts. Get it wrong, and the reverse is true.

Your business card represents you. Used to its fullest potential, a business card is not just contact information, it is far more – it's a mini business presentation. The greater the impact you can make on first contact with someone when you are networking, the better your chances are of standing out in the crowd and being memorable.

Key point

Your business card should be legible, succinct and contain a clear message. The recipient wants to see immediately from reading the card what services or products you provide.

Cards can be branded to reflect what you do and your position in the company. The card you hand to someone should be crisp and clean (not scruffy, dog-eared or dirty). Above all, it should look professional and be up to date with correct e-mail address, website details and contact numbers. Don't go with a design that is too arty or difficult to read. Some of the people you network with may not have 20/20 vision, even if you do. There is nothing worse than giving someone a card with printing so small it really needs an accompanying free magnifying glass.

The first thing is to decide on what the card needs to say. This may be something you can influence if you work for a small company. Should you be employed by a large corporation, this is probably a marketing or design department decision and your business card will be part of the corporate image and logo. Sometimes cards are brimming with information: your name, the company name, phone number, mobile number, fax number, direct dialling number, other branch offices, company logo, company slogan, mailing address, website. Is this all really necessary? Where should the emphasis be? On the website, for example, or on other information? Is the logo so strong that it is instantly recognizable? Or is the slogan the most important message to convey? Is working online so integral to your business that you don't need a geographical address any more? Once you know what's needed, make sure the style is clear. If you're keen to include a picture, make sure it's relevant. Your business card needs to give people the right information and be memorable. There's no value in them remembering you if they don't know how to contact you.

Key point

When you hand out a business card as you introduce yourself at meetings and networking events, it helps your new contact remember your name. By putting a business card into someone's hand you engage three senses while you have their attention: hearing, sight and touch. It conveys a powerful message.

In terms of networking activity, whether you are attending a social event, a trade exhibition, conference or seminar, the significance of business cards cannot be denied. They are the first visual representation people obtain of your company and services.

Don't forget it's not the quantity of cards that you hand out that matters. Quality counts not only in terms of the card and what it looks like, but in respect of the connections and relationships you are able to build from each and every occasion. The connection you create with someone during an event and a subsequent exchange of cards is a measurement of what you have accomplished in reaching your desired goal.

Returning to the practical point about card holders, it is worth investing in at least a couple of these. One is for keeping your own cards clean and fresh and the other can be for collecting the business cards given to you. Some people even have a third business card holder, in which they keep their credit or debit cards and driving licence. It's worth noting that in terms of personal security pickpockets don't expect cash or credit cards to be kept in a business card holder.

Why are they still necessary?

Many a small thing has been made large by the right kind of advertising.

Mark Twain

Business cards act as a tangible reminder of who you are and what you do. Used correctly, they could be earning you new business for years and years. Remember that in networking nothing is a quick fix. It takes time to build influential connections and a business card is a perfect aide memoire.

What do you do with all the business cards you've collected? How effective are they? Some people manage to amass hundreds of them. They end up stored in boxes, desk drawers, stapled to pieces of paper, stuck in the back of old diaries – anywhere but where they should be. The contact details you collect from people should be transferred to your electronic database as soon as possible, and a note section created so that you can record the date of the meeting and any follow-up action as it happens. If you don't do anything with the business cards you collect, how can they possibly work for you? Get them out of their hiding places and their data entered on to an Excel spreadsheet as fast as you can. They should be a networking aid, not a box full of memorabilia.

Key point

Unless you make other people's business cards work for you, you could be missing loads of opportunities to build relationships with people. This could have a dramatic impact on your business in respect of retaining existing clients or gaining new ones.

If you have a pile of cards you've collected over a long period of time, don't bin them because you're starting a new networking campaign. Go through them to see which of these contacts it's appropriate and worth touching base with. If you know something relevant and current about them, colour code the card (or database entry) to give you a clue. This could be as simple as a red mark if you've seen, spoken or done business with the person or company within the last three months. Orange could mean the contact is over six months old, green represents a year, and blue over two years. This is something you should make time to do – it's an unused and potentially valuable asset.

The ideal card and how to use it

Give them quality. That's the best kind of advertising.

M S Hershey

The ideal business card should look professional and have a unique corporate logo on it. If it is being designed for you, everything from style, font and graphic details should be cohesive and create an eye-catching and unforgettable snapshot of your brand image.

Case study

A newly formed catering company was proud of their logo and slogan. The branding had been created for them and their strap line was 'Snacks: healthy – interesting – tasty'. When it came to the design of their cards the initial letter S was large and printed in red, flowing like a ribbon. The other three initial letters, h, i and t, were also prominent. What a pity they hadn't realized that at first glance the word spelled by those initial letters wasn't particularly helpful in their chosen line of business. (This card was seen at a networking event; their business vehicles bore similar signage.)

The best way to exchange cards is by establishing rapport with someone in a conversation. If you aren't asked for your card, ask them first. Most people will respond. If they don't, say 'May I offer you one of my cards?' It is rare that you will get a refusal. When you are presented with someone's card, it is polite to look at it and then at the person. The Japanese art of exchanging business cards is an important tradition and is taken very seriously. You should make a comment about the card you've received. This is not only a polite acknowledgement but also will help you to remember both the card and the circumstances when you met the person. It is a crucial part of networking and makes the other person feel important.

You can always ask for referrals in this context, and this is dealt with in greater detail in Chapters 10 and 11. Referrals work in two ways: people feel more important if you ask them about referrals – you are paying them the compliment of asking their advice. People quite naturally respond to requests for help when asked. Don't forget to jot a few words on the back of cards you receive while at a networking event to aid recognition. Even if it's a scribbled note to remind you of a piece of information the person gave you (they've just moved to a town where you used to live), it can mean the difference between a follow-up happening or not.

Key point

If you can make someone feel important, you may be on the way to becoming important to them.

How will you be able to distinguish each individual whose cards you collected once you get back to work? If you want to be subtle, you could simply put the cards of people you definitely want to follow up with in one pocket and the others who may be less interesting in a different one. If you are networking with a specific target and have an appointment to meet someone, hand your business card to the receptionist or personal assistant when you arrive at their office. This helps in two ways: first, it ensures that your name is in full view and they are more likely to announce you correctly and second, your contact information is readily available for entering into their data system.

Key point

It sounds elementary, but do keep your own cards separate from the ones you collect. It can be embarrassing to be seen handing out other people's cards rather than your own – and it is easily done if you're a bit busy or disorganized.

Always carry your cards with you and have enough so that they are readily available when you need to pass them round. A box should be accessible in your bag, desk drawer or car. If the unthinkable should happen and you do run out of cards, best advice is to ask for a card from those you meet. Then make sure you e-mail them a quick note with your contact information within the next 24 hours, referring to the occasion when you met them.

Being creative with business cards is something quite simple but many people don't realize this. There is no need to stick with the small rectangular piece of white card with your name, company name and address plus a couple of contact numbers. Business cards can, and should, be diverse. You don't have to cling to something standard if you have the opportunity and ability to be creative.

Some businesses have successfully introduced loyalty cards – the ones where you get a hole punched each time you purchase something, so that after a certain number of visits you get something for free. This is just one example of creative use of a business card. It still carries the information about the store, or business, because the company name is prominently displayed on the card, acting as a continual reminder to go back again. But it is much more than just an address card. When someone carries a loyalty card, it encourages them to continue using that business outlet. Other companies use business cards as discounts or coupons – whatever it is, it's a good way to ensure the person carrying it will keep on returning to do business with them.

Other suggestions include 'thank you' cards, which you can hand out when someone has used your services. If you have lots of different services, a business card with all the services you offer printed on the back will remind people that there are other things they could use you for. This increases the likelihood of repeat work or extension work because they will be able to see everything that you do. Some companies offer magnetic cards so that they remain visible easily and act as a reminder of services that can be provided when you need them.

You might want to consider having your photo printed on your business card. Some people like to see who they are working with, and having an image of someone aids recognition. There is some evidence from recent research that seeing a photo on a business card and a website tends to help people develop rapport and trust faster than if there isn't a picture.

When you are going to a business event or networking gathering, research it a few days before. If you can, find out who will be attending so that you are able to meet those who may be potential clients or business partners. Depending on the size of the event, you will have a clue as to how many cards to take with you, but it is good practice to take more than you need. There are lots of different ways you can use business cards to draw in new prospects and sales. But before this chapter ends, here are a few things to avoid doing with your business cards.

Don't use free business cards. These are offered by a number of printing companies: their name is on the back while yours is on the front. The impression that this can convey is that you cannot afford proper business cards and you are promoting their company instead of your own.

As I have already mentioned, the printing on your business card should not be too small, nor should it be printed in colours that clash. Never use someone else's business card and scribble on it, or use an old business card with incorrect contact details. If you're getting new business cards printed, proofread the information carefully and double check the details. There is nothing worse than finding that the wrong information has been included. This is one of the quickest ways to lose potential business.

It isn't wise to have your business cards made larger than the standard size. Although they may stand out, it could mean your card doesn't fit into filing systems or wallets. To avoid being left out, stick to normal sizes but do be sure to choose a good-quality card with a reasonable weight of at least 250 gsm.

As an effective aid to networking, a business card should be distinctive enough for a new contact to remember the person who handed it out. The right business card will work harder for you than many of your staff. It is one of the vital tools for getting ahead in business. When you network online, your business card (your embedded signature) is visible on every communication. A good card should always be working for you, even when you aren't there. In terms of networking and building good relationships, it pays to have a business card and to use it to good effect.

6

First impressions

I don't possess a lot of self-confidence. I'm an actor, so I simply act confident every time I hit the stage.

Arsenio Hall

This chapter is about creating the right impression, building confidence and self-esteem not only in yourself but also in others. In terms of networking, these suggestions should help you develop your own style of sourcing new business contacts. One of the simplest and most successful ways is by being yourself and playing to your own personal strengths. The preceding chapter dealt with the role of business cards in creating a good impression. This one is about personal presentation and making a positive impact. It's worth bearing in mind that personal presentation has implications for networking in the virtual community too. You can give someone an impression (favourable or not) in many ways other than standing right in front of them. So take care with your online networking techniques too – they could be speaking volumes about you without you realizing it. In physical networking, within a few moments of meeting someone, assumptions and judgements are made. You know it's true – and it works both ways. However hard you try to avoid doing so, you're likely to make an instant decision about someone because of the way they look, speak or what they wear – and they're most probably doing the same about you.

In terms of how important networking is to your personal and business success, it's amazing how few people actually enjoy it or are good at it. It really isn't hard to do; politicians have to do it and become quite adept at it. When it comes to meeting new people, watch out for what you like in them. Human beings are quick to make judgements about others – it can take about eight seconds, that's all. Within that time you decide someone will be useful or fun or unfriendly, and whether you're going to continue a conversation with them or not. You'll even tense up with nerves if you want to impress them. This isn't a good way to start. People will react coolly towards you and you may miss opportunities to connect with great people who could be fun and make life even more interesting.

The next time you meet someone, focus on what you like about them and you will forge a connection right away. Perhaps you like how they introduced themselves, what they said to you, the way they looked, smiled, the tone of their voice or how they spoke or presented themselves. If you are sincere and genuinely interested in them this will have the effect of making you relax, and the other person will react positively towards you. The more you practise this, the easier it becomes, and you can feel the difference as it works. It really isn't difficult once you get the knack. Watching for what you like naturally about someone makes you more interesting. Being interested in someone means the exchange moves from stiff and formal into a more casual conversation, such as you would have with friends. Remember the key attributes of a successful networker? Curiosity (being interested in others); generosity (being a giver, not a taker); showing confidence (makes you seem trustworthy) and being motivated (having a purpose).

Key point

Remember – you never have a second chance to make a first impression.

There's a well known and often quoted statistic about making an entrance: 55 per cent of the impression you make is how you look (that is, posture and what you wear); 38 per cent is the energy and enthusiasm conveyed (by body language and tone of voice), and only 7 per cent is what you actually say to a person. This seems to indicate that visual impressions are more important than oral messages. Well that's okay, provided you get off to a good start: everything you do afterwards will just get that much easier. But what if you don't? A good beginning not only affects your business contact, it affects your confidence too. Start off a bit clumsily or shakily and there's no quicker way to zap your self-confidence. Confidence requires preparation and needs to be actively worked at to ensure you achieve the right impact.

You don't need to wait for someone to come to talk to you at a networking event. Even if you do feel shy or out of place at the beginning, remember that the other people are probably feeling much the same. Break the ice by approaching someone else who is standing on their own. Don't give way to feelings of inferiority. There could be experienced networkers at the event but you are all there for the same purpose – to make new friends. If you see someone networking effortlessly, that is because they have worked hard to perfect their own style. Follow their lead, be prepared to learn from others and forget about your own insecurity.

If you're well prepared you'll be more confident and better able to cope in networking situations. This has been mentioned already in terms of researching your opportunities, getting organized in relation to your database and how you keep track of your contacts. There's no magic formula for this, and it isn't a question of learning tricks or gimmicks. It's about being businesslike and professional and aware of the importance of everything going well in the early stages of building business relationships. Having the right intention is the first step towards achieving success.

Meeting and greeting – how to get it right

You have to have confidence in your ability, and then be tough enough to follow through.

Rosalynn Smith Carter

Creating the right impact is essential when you first meet someone. You can greatly influence the outcome of your networking experience by paying attention to certain details. Various situations require a different focus: for example, you would behave more informally at a party than when networking at a corporate event or in the boardroom. In the business environment your style of dress should show authority and inspire confidence – though you should look approachable too. The ideal image to create is that of cool self-assurance. Clothes matter and it's far safer to be well groomed, stylishly dressed and slightly conservative. Following the latest fashion trend isn't necessary when networking in a business setting. Designer labels are great if that's your style, but they are not essential. Aim to have well-manicured hands, clean, well-cut hair and good-quality accessories. If the overall impression is that you are well groomed, then you're a winner.

Don't forget your feet – you may be standing for a long time. If possible, you should avoid wearing a new pair of shoes to an important business function. What if, for instance, your shoes pinch or have four-inch heels (and that includes the men)? You won't be able to stand or walk comfortably in them. Find another pair. Be less ambitious and err on the side of comfort. Who knows, you might be invited to accompany someone on a tour of the whole of their new corporate headquarters, or be kept standing for ages while waiting to meet someone at a reception line-up. Aching feet are the last thing you need when you are trying to look good and appear relaxed at the same time.

There is one characteristic that everyone possesses and can always be used to advantage when networking. A lot of people take it for granted or forget to use it. It will draw people towards you, they will respond positively and it can help ease you into a conversation. It's been used by people for centuries and is understood by every culture in the world and by every person, no matter how old they are or how important. If you use it every day, the number of new friends you make will increase rapidly. You can start (or end) a conversation with it and it is a great waste of a valuable resource to conceal it. If you practise using it, people will remember you and tell others about you. It can change the energy in a room and lighten people's moods. It communicates your personality and leaves a lasting impression. You can even use it on the phone.

What is it? It's your smile.

Key point

One of the easiest ways to outshine everyone and appear charming is to smile.

Many people have the most wonderful natural smiles, but due to nervousness or apprehension, all that seems to be registering on their faces are the stress muscles.

A smile lights up a face – so use yours to good effect. People who smile give the impression of being pleasant, attractive, sincere and confident. It relaxes those with whom you are making contact and usually results in a 'mirroring' gesture from them.

Good manners never go amiss – that applies in every networking situation. If you have an appointment, be punctual. The overriding impression should be that you are capable of arriving somewhere on time. If you turn up late, whatever the reason, all that your new contact will remember is that you weren't there on time. It could mean that your first encounter will be your last.

However organized you are, allow yourself extra time if you are travelling to a networking event, to avoid stress. If you arrive in a fluster and out of breath, you'll be in the wrong frame of mind to get the most out of the occasion. Appearing cool, calm and collected is well worth the extra investment of a taxi ride, if that's all it takes.

It may seem unnecessary to point this out, but it is surprising how many people can't help their eyes straying should an interruption occur. If you are engaged in conversation with someone, keep your eyes and ears directed towards them at all times. If you can create the impression that they have all your attention, you will have made excellent progress towards building a positive impression. There is nothing more encouraging for someone than to be made to feel important. You are likely to be placed high in their estimation if you can develop this skill.

Another vital rule in any social or business networking encounter: make sure your mobile phone is switched off. There's no better way to kill off goodwill than being interrupted by a ringtone coming from your pocket or bag. This applies the other way round too. If someone you are speaking to has the insensitivity to receive calls and messages throughout your meeting, at the very least it is an insult. It shows a lack of respect for you and creates completely the wrong impression. There are a few occasions when such interruptions are unavoidable. But if you happen to be talking to someone while expecting an important call, have the courtesy to tell them so. If the phone call does interrupt your dialogue, explain politely that it's the call you were expecting, and could they excuse you for a moment while you respond. Make a discreet exit – and be brief.

Provided you have a reasonable amount of self-esteem, you should be able to conduct yourself in a networking situation in a favourable and positive way. Don't start networking in situations where you know you will lack confidence. Do you know what impression you convey to people at a first meeting? If not, ask someone who knows you well and is prepared to tell you the truth.

If you have tried networking before, how do existing contacts react towards you? Are there any behavioural traits you portray that might be worth changing? Depending on the information you have, concentrate on a positive mental attitude. Behave and look as if you have already achieved your goals. Confidence breeds confidence and as it develops, it will become natural to you and you will have a positive impact on others.

It doesn't matter who you are, people will make judgements based on their first impressions. One of the key reasons why you need to spend time and effort on your appearance is to give yourself that confidence boost so that you feel self-assured. Once you've achieved this, there'll be no holding you back. Remember that the outcome of many situations is often determined by the confidence shown by the parties involved. A lack of skill or knowledge can go unnoticed. A conflict can be resolved or a business contract won purely through a display of confidence. Self-belief and self-assurance are vital if you are to realize your potential and get rewards from your networking. By challenging your thinking and working on the areas that need adapting, you can make a positive start. Confidence is like a muscle – it needs to be worked on to be developed.

Presentation skills – a quick guide

Use what talents you possess. The woods would be very silent if no birds sang except those that sang best.

Henry Van Dyke

Your appearance is really important in networking – after all, it is your personal brand. People judge you on the way you look, so make sure it's as good as possible. If you don't know what to wear, get some advice. If name tags are being used, make sure yours is in a visible place. Clean clothes, polished shoes, a decent pen, smart portfolio, tidy hair, go easy on the perfume or aftershave – all these things, and more, need to be on your presentation checklist.

It's worth spending a moment or two on yours to see which areas need a bit of attention. Ask a close friend if they could help by saying what they think you are good at, and what things might improve with some attention. For example, lots of people sit slouched at their computers for hours. This is one of the most common mistakes where personal deportment is concerned but it's a bad habit many get into. One tip from the experts is to imagine a golden thread running from the top of your head to the ceiling. When you stand or sit, imagine this thread is pulling you upright. You will grow taller and instantly become more noticeable.

Since posture and body language are both important when it comes to personal presentation, if you think you need help on this one, and want to come across as a professional, it might be worth investing in some personal presentation training. Some companies offer this as standard for staff employed in customer-facing roles. Why not enquire whether your organization would be able to arrange this for you? Some presentation skills trainers start by making a video of the way you walk, talk, stand and sit, and how you present yourself at meetings and corporate events. This is a fairly harsh way of finding out all your weak points, but it does focus the mind and help you address these areas swiftly and effectively. Even if you don't have the opportunity to get professional assistance, there is a lot you can do to help yourself.

Whether or not you are a shy type, meeting people who show signs of nerves or low self-esteem can be off-putting. Things to watch out for are restless people, those fidgeting with clothes, hair or jewellery (their own, hopefully), gripping their hands tightly, lowering their head and generally avoiding eye contact. It's a natural instinct when you're apprehensive to want to make yourself smaller, so people who cross their arms or hold their bags in front of them convey anxiety and timidity.

Controlling your arms gives powerful clues as to how confident, open and receptive you are. Keeping your arms relaxed and by the sides of your body shows you are not scared. You give the impression of being able to take whatever comes your way: meeting things 'full frontal'. The more outgoing you are, the more likely that you'll use your arms to great effect, with big movements and gestures. If you're the quiet type, you move your limbs less and keep them close to your body. Hands should be still, unless they are being used to create expressive gestures. A good idea is to look at the behaviour of politicians – you can usually spot those who've had the presentation skills training, and those who haven't.

Key point

If you want to be seen as a confident and self-assured person, capable of networking effectively in a cool professional manner, using open body language will make you more persuasive.

Open body language means you are not fearful in other people's company. Those who stand upright, balanced on both feet with their weight evenly distributed, show that they are in control. Remember that the body is an instrument – it can convey every emotion. Watch people who use mirroring gestures. This is something used to great effect by people who want to create a good first impression with new business contacts. Copying what someone else does (provided it is a positive and not a negative action) endorses the favourable view they've formed of you. This reinforces the right impression and creates a bond between the parties.

It is often said that actions speak louder than words, and body language speaks volumes. When you are trying to create a favourable impression with someone, your body will quite naturally point towards them: your face, hands, arms, feet and legs. These gestures can be quite subconscious. But they are picked up easily by the other person. If you've ever thought about this, you've probably noticed it dozens of times among people you've sat next to at work, when travelling or in social situations.

Try watching next time you've got a few moments to spare – observe how individuals position themselves when communicating with each other. You'll notice how they naturally angle themselves towards the person on whom they are trying to create a positive impression, and turn away from those they are seeking to avoid.

Key point

Making the correct eye contact when networking is important. Usually you are dealing with someone you don't know very well, so there are a number of things to remember regarding the eyes and the head.

It is quite natural to look at people from eye to eye and across the top of the nose. This is the safe area to which eye contact should be confined. With friends, in social situations, this area of vision increases to include both eyes but also downwards to the nose and mouth. When you flirt with someone, the scope of this triangle increases – widening at the base to involve more of the body. If you're very nervous, try not to stare obsessively at someone when they are speaking to you. They could be forgiven for thinking that there's something wrong with their face, and become rather anxious. On the other hand, looking away completely, slow blinking or closing the eyes for longer periods than normal can be a clear indication of lack of interest, or worse, boredom. Keeping your head level both horizontally and vertically gives the impression of authority, while a friendly gesture is to tilt your head slightly to one side or the other while listening to someone speak.

One very important point to remember is that you were given two ears and only one mouth – so use them in that proportion. If you can spend twice as much time listening as you do talking, you will be creating a positive impression. (There's more information on listening skills in the next chapter). People will regard you as a skilled communicator who knows how to initiate a conversation without dominating it.

Starting as you mean to go on

You've got to take the initiative and play your game. In a decisive set, confidence makes the difference.

Christine Marie Evert

So you've decided to get started on your networking strategy – well done. Before you take things a stage further, it's worth mentioning that wherever you are, whatever you do, the un-expected may happen. This refers to positive as well as negative occurrences. With regard to life's bonuses, you should be prepared to meet people who are interesting and who could, at some point, have a lot of influence in your life. This could be in either your social or your professional life. To get best results, looking, acting and feeling positive will help.

Key point

If you feel apprehensive about getting involved with new people, or striking out into unknown territory, remember – be safe. If you take sensible precautions, you can reduce the fear factor considerably.

Whether you are networking for pleasure or for professional rea-sons, you'd be wise to make sure someone knows where you are, what event or venue you're attending. This is simple common sense. If you've decided to go to an event connected with work, someone in the office should be aware of your arrangements. If, on the other hand, you've decided to take up a new hobby as a means of getting to know more people, tell a friend, relative or neighbour if you are going off to a meeting or gathering some distance away. If possible, let them know who you're with. Always leave a contact number and give them some idea of when you'll be back. This may seem over-cautious, but it is better to be prepared than regret it later. If you take sensible precautions, you will probably never need them.

If you like making lists, you could start by checking the following things that you should consider. These include making sure you have enough money to get a taxi cab home if needed; sufficient fuel in your car to drive to and from your destination without grinding to a halt; enough charge on your mobile phone battery to call someone if you are unavoidably delayed or stuck on public transport. If the networking event is activity related, there are other things too. For example, if you're going on a long trek as part of a team-building exercise with colleagues at work, take the appropriate clothing and equipment. Anyone doing something for the first time can all too easily be taken unawares. You could get cold, wet, hot or hungry if you are stranded for any length of time. This applies whether you are in the city or the country.

Another point to consider: the cost implications. You may have plenty of time to invest, because your chosen networking activities can be done after work or at weekends. But don't go over the top and join a club that's for the super-rich, if you're not one of them. Some sports, for example, are best left to tycoons. You won't get far trying to network in a private flying club if you can't afford to buy or charter a plane. Even if you're thinking of taking up golf, there are some very expensive clubs where the subscription levels, joining fees and equipment need fairly deep pockets. These tend to be full of people who have healthy amounts of disposable income. Getting to know them would simply mean you might have trouble maintaining the connections. If golf is something you've always wanted to take up and are keen to make new friends on the circuit, join a club by all means, but choose one that fits comfortably within your budget. It should not bring with it any financial worries about keeping your membership going and affording the green fees.

Key point

If your networking strategy involves sports, hobbies or special-interest groups, these should be for fun and help reduce stress levels, not increase them.

Whatever your choice, start modestly and keep investment to a minimum early on in the proceedings.

Case study

Maria wanted to meet interesting, artistic and intelligent people. She decided to invest in a number of expensive tickets for the national opera house. She was excited the first time she attended a performance, but as soon as the diva opened her mouth Maria felt ill. The noise brought on an instant migraine and she had to leave. This was as disappointing as it was unhelpful. Maria had had no idea she was noise sensitive. The whole effort proved a complete disaster, as she was unable to resell her tickets and had to give them away. The next time she tried social networking she made certain she didn't invest money up front, to be sure that should she need to she could make a quick and easy exit without regretting it bitterly.

Should you meet someone at a networking event with whom you get on well, resist the temptation to divulge loads of personal information on first acquaintance. It's equally inappropriate to question anyone deeply about their lifestyle, previous relationships or, worse, their assets, or political or religious views. Personal safety issues are paramount however you are attempting to network, including online (see Chapter 4). Networking isn't regarded as a high-risk activity, but you should always act responsibly and avoid situations that look potentially troublesome. This will keep you clear of trouble.

When you arrive at your networking event, however apprehensive you are, don't overindulge – whether on drink or any other substances. You may think a quick fix will help you relax, but there is nothing less attractive than a pleasant and potentially interesting person losing control during the evening. If you're trying to create a good first impression, this is the worst thing you can do. No matter how nervous you are, don't use stimulants to get you through. Deep breathing is simpler and far safer.

The same applies to eating – a smart dinner is not an opportunity to see how much gourmet food you can shovel down your throat. The way people eat speaks volumes about what they are like. If you want to pass the dining test, your table manners should be impeccable. If you're invited to a dinner, accept graciously. If you're a student who's been living on rice and tinned tomatoes for months, it may be a free meal but don't go berserk. It's far better to eat sparingly and delicately than behave like a child let loose in a sweet shop. Should you be unsure what to choose, and the restaurant or menu is unfamiliar, ask for help. No one will mind your lack of knowledge. You could ask your host what they recommend, or request the waiters to assist you. If in doubt, keep to simple dishes with standard cutlery.

There are some delicious foods available – but some can be a touch complicated as to how you get them from the plate into your mouth. With a formal dinner, if you're not sure how to eat a particular course, you can watch to see how the person on your left, right or opposite you tackles it – assuming they're eating the same thing. It is embarrassing (but not unknown) to be caught drinking out of the finger bowl or using the wrong implements for the different courses. You will soon learn.

Another simple but essential rule: don't talk with your mouth full. Even if you have something really witty to say, it pays to hold back. Nothing spoils an occasion faster than spraying the person you're talking to with half-eaten morsels. If this does happen, do restrain yourself from leaning towards the person to pick the bits of food off their clothes. That will only make matters worse. Let them do it.

Finally, a word about how to be irresistible. Many people miss the subtleties and distinguishing factors in life that can make a whole world of difference. If someone is described as *knowledgeable*, you'd be absolutely right to assume that they know quite a lot and are fairly intelligent. However, if they are described as *wise*, think about it, there's a whole lot more meaning to that word. It indicates that the person certainly has knowledge, but applies it in a way that creates a much greater effect. A knowledgeable person tells you, with little encouragement, what they know. A wise person knows a great deal but doesn't bombard you, applying their wisdom as and when necessary. It's much more interesting to talk to a wise person than to a knowledgeable one.

Consider the difference between the words *lonely* and *solitary*. If someone is lonely, the inference is that they are on their own and would much rather not be. If on the other hand someone is described as solitary, it could be that they just enjoy their own company and find it refreshing to have time to themselves without other distractions. Lonely has negative connotations, while solitary can be used simply descriptively. Make sure when you are networking that you encourage the lonely person out of their shyness if that is something you can do. But if someone is solitary (contemplating an artwork or a magnificent view or sunset) it is not always appropriate to interrupt them and engage them in small talk. If you really feel you must do so, wait until they turn around or are about to move out of their reverie.

Where networking is concerned, think about these similar words: *talkative* and *conversational*. A talkative person probably chatters away quite happily, unaware of their listener's feelings.

A conversational person, on the other hand, has awareness of the other person and understands that speech is a two-way thing. A conversational person draws their audience in, allows them to react, reflect and respond to what they are saying. It's a far pleasanter experience to network with a conversationalist than with a talker. Which one would you rather be described as?

Then have a think about being *friendly* and *welcoming*. What's the subtle difference here? If you are a friendly person, you probably smile when you meet someone and say hello. After this you may move on to greet someone else. A welcoming type on the other hand is a much warmer character and acts in a deeper way. The greeting is followed by a polite enquiry: 'How was your journey?' 'Have you had a good meeting?' The friendly person may talk easily to someone when networking but the welcoming person actively works to find a connection, something in common that makes the exchange memorable. In a word, the welcoming person makes you feel special because they are thinking about you – not about themselves.

The instances above are worth considering because it is important to get networking right. Done well, it has far-reaching rewards and as your face-to-face networking forays become more frequent, you will become more confident and things will get easier. Relax – your social outings should be memorable for all the right reasons, and you can become irresistible too.

7

The art of conversation

To listen closely and reply well is the highest perfection we are able to attain in the art of conversation.
François de la Rochefoucauld (1613–1680)

The previous chapter dealt with the importance of making a good impression – how appearance and body language can make or break the first few seconds of an initial encounter. Now you've reached the point when you're about to speak to some new contacts at a networking event. Conversation is an art, communication is an ability. In this chapter the habits of skilled communicators are discussed along with some advice on how best to conduct a conversation. The most important thing to bear in mind in networking is that other people matter – not just *you*. The art of conversation is a two-way process – you will need to be able to switch confidently between 'transmitting' and 'receiving' modes. In relation to networking in the virtual community, there are many distinctions to be made. Online conversations in chat rooms or website forums tend to be informal, relaxed and casual. In general in this chapter it is assumed that you wish to develop good face-to-face conversational techniques for use in professional networking situations.

Key point

In conversation it's best to aim for dialogue, not a monologue.

One-to-one meetings can result in awkward pauses and initial shyness for those who aren't confident. To come across well to someone, think about what you would like to achieve during the dialogue. What information do you wish to convey? What information would you ideally like to receive? What do you want the other person to do as a result? Organize yourself beforehand, be positive and keep the message simple. Communication in essence is signalling. It's the transmission, by speaking, writing or gestures, of information that evokes understanding. Now that's straightforward enough, but in practice it can be more difficult – particularly if you have high expectations from the conversations you plan to conduct. In order for an oral exchange to become a conversation, something else has to occur. The other party has to engage the brain, receive the message and respond. Moreover, you must pay attention to what is said.

Whether you're new to attending networking events or not, you do need to have something to talk about when you meet someone. Obviously you'll share who you are and what you do, but the goal must be to get them to talk about themselves. Everyone loves to talk about themselves, especially if someone shows a genuine interest. In order to create the best possible impression, you should engage with them and listen carefully. Asking about what they enjoy doing is one way to start. You should be looking for something to connect with them about, so that you can share a mutual interest. The focus should always be on them, not you. Sincerity counts and a compliment never goes amiss.

What to say and how to be memorable

You impress folks that little bit more with what you're saying if you say it nicely. People don't hear your ideas if you just stand there shouting out the words.

Lord Gormley

When you are starting a conversation, remember one of the key attributes of a successful networker: curiosity. Add to that the ability to ask open questions, which require an explanation in terms of an answer, and you have a winning formula.

If you think you may stumble at first, try to remember that if you ask questions about the following subjects you will be *FINE*: Family, Interests, News, Employment. Most people will happily talk about their family, so an introductory question on this subject is not going to be difficult for you. Asking someone about their interests or hobbies is another perfectly acceptable line of enquiry, so no worries here either. News? Well, most people have an opinion on current affairs or local events, so a casual mention about an item that been reported on the local, national or international news could work. You don't want to start off with a remark that would open a heated debate, as if you were at the dispatch box in Parliament. There is so much emphasis on pop culture today, there's bound to be an opportunity to mention some celebrity or other who has just done something amazing or crass; it's another opening gambit. Finally, employment: most people are willing to tell you what they do for a living. This is the one you are probably most interested in anyway if you are networking for professional reasons. Even the most nervous among us should be able to remember *FINE* when we walk into a room full of strangers. Don't worry if you mix up the order of the letters and you end up asking your questions in a different sequence – just use the word as a mnemonic and get started.

Humour can be a wonderful ice breaker. Don't try telling risqué jokes – that won't work. But introducing some fun into the conversation is always helpful. People who are naturally amusing draw others towards them like a magnet. Just because you have a sense of humour doesn't mean you aren't professional or serious about doing business.

To be successful, you need to know when and how to strike up a conversation. When you've attended a few networking events you'll have seen how best to move around a room, mix and mingle and introduce yourself to new people. Remember to study the body language of people talking. If they're facing each other and passionately debating a point, it is unlikely that you will be welcome intruding into their space. It's a different matter if you see people making small talk and scanning the room, ready to meet someone else's gaze. In that situation it is perfectly acceptable to approach them and say hello.

Do you remember in the previous chapter on first impressions, only 7 per cent of the impact you make comes from the words you speak? The remaining 93 per cent comes from visual aspects: appearance, sound of voice and body language. Did you know that you can break that 7 per cent down even further by considering the type of words you use, the sort of sentences you use and how you phrase them?

Key point

Making a favourable impression on a potential new business contact requires careful consideration of the words, the ideas and structure of the message you wish to convey. Keep it simple if you possibly can.

Always aim for clarity over ambiguity. For example, commonly used words, in short direct sentences, have the greatest impact and allow the least margin for error or misinterpretation. Long words wrapped in complex sentences are confusing and best avoided. Don't use jargon unless you know the other party will understand it (for example, because you both work in the same field or profession). Positive statements are far more acceptable and will gain you greater advantage than negatively expressed remarks. If, due to nerves, you manage early on in an exchange to insert both feet into your mouth with great speed and agility, you won't be the first person to have come unstuck when trying to initiate a conversation. Sometimes thing go wrong before you've had time to sit down.

Without going any further, let's first consider one of the most important aspects of the conversational process. This is your voice: the tone, inflection, volume and pitch are all areas you must think about. Most people don't need to develop their speaking voice because it is a pleasant and natural asset (like a smile). But some people don't understand how to use it effectively. The simplest way is to compare the voice to a piece of music – it is the instrument of interpretation of the spoken word. Those who have had the benefit of training in public speaking, or have had some singing lessons, sometimes use mnemonics as memory joggers for best vocal effect. One simple example is *RSVPPP* – which stands for Rhythm, Speed, Voice, Pitch, Pause and Projection.

Rhythm. Speaking without variety of tone can anaesthetize your listener. Try raising and lowering the voice to bring vocal sound to life (and keep your audience awake). Rhythm is directly linked with speed.

Speed. Speed variation is connected to the vocal rhythm. Varying speed makes for interested listeners and helps them maintain concentration. If you're recounting a story, speed helps to add excitement to the tale. But the speed of delivery should be matched with the volume you're speaking at.

Volume. Level of volume obviously depends on where the conversation is taking place. It would be inappropriate to use loud volume when speaking in a one-to-one situation. However, you'd probably need to increase it if you were talking in a crowded venue, such as a business reception or work area. Volume is used mainly for emphasis and to command attention – lowering your voice can add authority when telling an interesting story or giving advice.

Pitch. Pitching your voice is something public speakers do. They are trained to 'throw' their voices so they can deliver their speech clearly to their audience in whatever size or shape of room they're speaking in. In general, it's irritating to any listener if they have to strain to hear what the speaker is saying. In normal conversations where you need to be heard clearly (for example, in restaurants where there is continual background noise as well as the hubbub of other voices) it's impossible to pitch your voice if you hardly open your mouth to let the words out. Correct use of mouth, jaw and lip muscles will produce correctly accentuated words and assist with clear enunciation. Pay attention to these facial muscles, otherwise your voice may sound monotonous.

Pause. Practise the pause. It can be the most effective use of your voice, though it is often ignored. A pause should last about four seconds. Perhaps this sounds like an eternity, but anything shorter will go unnoticed by your listener. You can use the time to maintain good eye contact. The effect can be dynamite. Remember the 'er' count: filling spaces in conversation with props such as 'er', 'um' or 'you know', particularly where there should be pauses, is a clear sign of nervousness.

Projection. This encompasses everything about the way you come across: power, personality, weight, authority, and expertise – what some people call 'clout'. You want to build some long-lasting powerful business connections. It pays to have some gravitas in your dealings with people. Projection is an art that can be practised and you can learn a good deal from listening to experienced communicators, so take whatever opportunities you can to do this.

Key point

Your voice is an instrument, like your body – it's flexible. You know the expression 'It's not what you say, it's the way that you say it.' Bear that in mind when starting a conversation.

Perhaps a colleague or a friend would agree to give you feedback on your voice and mannerisms if you are unsure how you sound. Unless you get an accurate appraisal, you could be spoiling your chances of successful networking opportunities. With a bit of practice you'll be surprised how quickly bad habits can be replaced with good ones. This improvement in your style of conversation will increase your self-confidence when meeting people. Best advice: be clear – use simple, easily understood words and phrases; be loud (enough) so that your listener can hear you; be assertive – a bright and confident tone will inject interest into anything you're saying. Do stop for breath, pause to let your listener digest what you've said, and switch from transmitting to receiving mode.

This is a two-way operation

I wish people who have trouble communicating would just shut up.
Tom Lehrer

The key to success is to get on the other person's wavelength as soon as possible. Put yourself in their shoes and demonstrate your ability to empathize. This way your new contact will find communicating with you easy and respond positively. One important aspect of the art of conversation is developing good listening skills. Remember what I said in the previous chapter about why you have two ears and one mouth – so that you listen twice as much as you speak. By listening you will pick up quickly on the areas of common ground between you. A lot of people don't listen all that well.

If you're far more interested in what you have to say than anything else, your conversation won't get off to a very good start. Poor listening ability limits the chance of a positive result in a networking situation. Learn to listen attentively and you'll be successful.

A good listener is someone who keeps a comfortable level of eye contact and has an open and relaxed but alert pose. You should face the speaker and respond to what they are saying with appropriate facial expressions, offering encouragement with a nod or a smile. Adopting the behaviour of a good listener will help you establish instant rapport with your business contact. It requires a degree of self-discipline and a genuine desire to take on board the message the speaker is trying to convey. You need to be able to suspend judgement and avoid contradicting or interrupting them. Postpone saying your bit until you are sure the other person has finished and you have understood their point. Reflecting and summarizing – repeating back a key word or phrase the speaker has used – shows you have listened and understood. Summarizing gives the speaker a chance to add to or amend your understanding. Your networking contact is far more likely to listen to you if you demonstrate you've heard what they said by using these tactics.

Some tips on what to avoid: thinking up clever counter arguments before the speaker has finished making their point; interrupting unnecessarily or reacting emotionally to anything that is said. If the subject becomes dull or complex, don't register your disinterest by succumbing to distractions or fidgeting.

In case you're not familiar with them, here is a summary of the five levels of listening skills. The first and worst level is ignoring the speaker. You look away, avoid eye contact and do something else altogether. This is dreadful in a business context. Your hard-earned networking opportunity will evaporate instantly if you do this.

The second level, which is almost as bad, is to pretend to listen. In some ways this can be quite dangerous. If you're nodding your head, and saying 'Mmm, yes, aha' when you actually have no idea what's being said, you could be in for a surprise. Don't be shocked if you hear the other person saying 'So you'll run in the London Marathon next year on behalf of my favourite charity – how wonderful!'

The third level of listening skill is being selective. You may well find yourself listening for key words that are of importance, such as 'new project', 'budgets' or 'work opportunity'. The result is that you miss the main content of the exchange. Your contact could have been telling you that there are no openings for new business until the end of next year.

If you can develop the fourth level of skill, you're doing well. This is called being attentive. You are focused, with positive body language, leaning forward, nodding your head appropriately and maintaining eye contact. The other person knows you're paying attention and this creates an atmosphere where they'll want to share valuable information and engage in serious dialogue.

The fifth and highest level is empathetic. Empathy is the ability to think in the same way as someone else and see things from their perspective. It is the art of being able to identify mentally and emotionally with your communicator; fully comprehending the tones, pitch, body language and other subtle messages they are conveying. It's totally exhausting to do this for any length of time but it will take your business relationship to a high level if you can do it. You can't do this in a hurry – many meetings will have to take place before you reach this stage. You will have included each other in the closest of possible personal networks (sometimes called a virtual team). The other person will consider you one of their first ports of call when information gathering or project awarding is required, and you'll willingly reciprocate.

Key point

If you can build rapport with your networking contact you will be making great progress in establishing the relationship you want. Subsequent exchanges will become more relaxed and valuable.

Can you recall a time when you've been chatting to a work colleague, or a friend, and you've looked at your watch and said 'Wow, is that the time? I must have been talking to you for ages.' This usually happens when the two people concerned are giving each other space in their conversation. There is a feeling of ease, ideas are being passed to and fro, and a natural exchange develops. Conversation is a bit like a friendly game of tennis.

There are times when you'll want to find out more information while networking. It's easy to ask too many questions and fall into a sort of 'Spanish Inquisition' situation. Conversely, when responding to a question you can give more information than is necessary. If you're on the receiving end of this from your business contact, the relationship may not make much progress. No one likes to feel they are being 'pumped' for information. It's infuriating and insulting and you'll want to distance yourself as quickly as possible.

Key point

Only one person at a time can truly direct a conversation. One leads and the other tends to follow. This doesn't mean there's no give and take. Neither does it mean that the other party is subservient.

When starting a conversation, there are usually some general opening remarks. Watch for the moment when small talk ceases. At this point one of you should lead the exchange in the appropriate direction. That person should be you. If you don't seize the opportunity you may lose the initiative for the rest of the exchange. Consider planning a short agenda if you think you'll need a checklist – even if only in your head. This could mean that you have an element of control during the dialogue, should the conversation meander along. You could say something like 'It would be helpful to have a word about...' and then move on smoothly to the next stage. The initial stage of any conversation requires confidence. You'll feel and operate better if you get off to a planned start and you'll be able to maintain better control in directing the rest of the dialogue.

Why conversation matters

Are you planning to become an expert networker because you aim to be a high achiever or are you just looking to meet some new, interesting people and overcome your natural shyness? Whatever your reason, dealing with face-to-face encounters with strangers is a tough test. Any direct meeting – for whatever purpose – can result in awkward pauses and initial apprehension. Even worse, you may stumble over your words, feel and act clumsily because of nerves. Foot-in-mouth syndrome is a common occurrence; even among experienced communicators it happens from time to time (proven by some hilarious out-takes and howlers from commentators and presenters that appear on our TV screens). Don't worry about it, everyone makes mistakes.

To recap. Communication is signalling: the transmission, by speaking, writing or gestures, of information that evokes understanding. To achieve a conversation, the other party has to receive the message, understand it and respond.

Key point

One well-known example of communication failure is that of the swimmer who went too far from the shore, got into difficulties and drowned. The man on the beach who had watched the whole scene said afterwards, 'But I thought he was waving, not drowning.'

To develop a balanced style of communication, try to begin the conversation by introducing yourself and giving some personal information. This is called the inform stage. Once you've given some information, ask a direct question of your networking contact. This is called the invite stage. Then wait for their response. On receiving this, listen carefully. Then acknowledge and, if necessary, repeat the essence of their response. If you achieve this cycle of communication you can repeat it many times over during the encounter to establish a good rapport between you both. It should enable the conversation to flow, help the time pass effortlessly and harmoniously and make your networking experience a pleasant one.

Let us make a special effort to stop communicating with each other, so we can have some conversation.

Judith Martin (Miss Manners)

Networking has similarities to the dating process. Perhaps that is why speed dating and speed networking events have developed. You are attempting to get closer to a new contact by means of good conversation, so pay attention to the eye contact. This has been covered in the previous chapter, but it is so important it is worth recapping here. Appropriate eye contact at networking events is essential. If your contact is looking at you with an interested expression while you're talking, you're holding their attention. They may be nodding occasionally, smiling at times, and have an alert and open posture.

Here are some things to look out for if they aren't. Should they find it difficult to keep their eyes open during one of your conversational gambits, it could mean that they've had a late night; or they've had an early start; or they're suffering from jet lag; or they're nervous and have taken too many tranquillizers; or the atmosphere in the room is too stuffy; or... your dialogue is boring them. Don't wait until their head falls forward and hits you on the chest. Stop talking and see if they respond.

Keep an eye out for someone who fidgets while you're talking to them. This could indicate that you've lost their attention; or they're hoping for an interruption; or they're irritated by something you've said; or... they find the conversation irrelevant. Whatever the reason, it's time to shut up. Hopefully, with a pause you can retrieve a business relationship that's got off to a shaky start.

If the new contact starts shaking their head, this could mean they want to say something; or they don't agree with you; or... they simply don't have a clue what you're waffling on about. Again, time to bring your remarks to a swift close.

If you think you've lost the other person's attention completely and they've turned off, try to regain ground by asking a pertinent question. Establish eye contact again and vary the volume or expression in your voice.

You may have to conduct a networking exchange over the telephone. For inexperienced conversationalists, this could be difficult to deal with. Misunderstandings can occur between parties who do not know each other all that well. The main reason is obvious: because you can't see each other face to face, you have to rely on tone of voice. This is often deceptive. The caller may sound disinterested because they're talking in a low voice. It may be something as simple as the fact that they've got a sore throat or they're trying to prevent the rest of the office hearing their conversation. It's essential to pay attention when your new business contact is on the phone. If they're on a bad line or speaking on a mobile in a poor reception area, you may well get distortion, background noise, passing traffic, airport announcements or similar. If possible, take the phone call in a private place so as to avoid even more noise coming from your end of the phone.

Voicemail messages are another tricky issue. There's an art to leaving successful voicemail messages. It's simply this: be clear and be concise; don't speak too fast. If you are leaving your telephone number, slow down. Speak slowly while recording the information. If the message you leave is either gabbled or garbled, it will make it difficult for anyone to return your call. Remember to leave a date and time when you record your message, so that your contact can respond quickly if time is critical.

Text messages are a perfect form of communication for quick exchanges of information. One word of warning, though: don't use confusing abbreviations. If you received the following message with regard to a theatre trip – 'cu 7.30' – what would you think it meant? 'See you at 7.30 pm' or 'Curtain up at 7.30 pm'? Ambiguous or what?

> *The secret of success is sincerity. Once you can fake that you've got it made.*
>
> Jean Giraudoux (1882–1944)

Where conversation is concerned, it pays to get it right. There's such a lot that can result from a successful exchange when networking. Pay attention to the way your voice and body language are used in conjunction with the words you speak. You can convey the right impression if they are used correctly. Don't underestimate the importance of new relationships; you should try to get on the same wavelength of your business prospect as soon as possible. When engaged in conversation with your networking contact, make sure you match your question to the situation or subject. Beware of asking irrelevant questions; this will show that you've not paid attention to what they said. Listen attentively. Try to reach at least the fourth level of listening skill. Develop the habit of glancing at your networking contact to see that they're still engaged with the dialogue. Watch for mirroring gestures, as these indicate good rapport. Finally, remember the 'er' count. Reflecting and summarizing – repeating back a key word or phrase the speaker has used – show you have listened and understood. If the subject becomes dull or complex, don't show your disinterest by succumbing to distractions or fidgeting.

A word of warning: never bring up someone else in a conversation if you've had a negative experience with them. Another thing: avoid engaging in gossip. After you've been networking a while you'll find out how connected people really are (if you're not already familiar with the concept of six degrees of separation, see Chapter 10) and how regularly coincidences occur. Should you be in a situation where someone has told you where they work, and you say that you know someone in that firm, don't add 'not that they ever do any work, mind you'. You never know, these two people may be colleagues and good friends. You could have lost yourself a new business contact by one careless and inappropriate comment. Talk in general terms and don't mention any names; it's not worth the risk.

There is a likelihood that you might at some point try to communicate with someone the wrong way. You could be a person who wants to get to the point quickly, because you are business-like, professional and hate to waste time. Other people may not work that way and prefer to take time and have everything spelled out for them. Be aware of different personality types and remember the mirroring effect – copying their way of doing things is often the best way to get them to receive information. If they talk slowly, reduce the speed at which you speak. If they are a 'bottom line' person like you, you can cut to the chase right away.

Good conversation is as stimulating as black coffee – and just as hard to sleep after.
Anne Morrow Lindbergh (*Gift from the Sea*)

If there is a golden rule in the art of conversation, it is to start by finding a common thread. Whether it's the fact that you live in the same area of the city, or you've both been drenched in the sudden storm reaching the venue, it doesn't matter. You have the event and the group in common, so enquire if the other person has been to the venue before. Should they have a friend or acquaintance attending the event, ask if they'd mind introducing you to them.

Don't apologize. Just because you're nervous is no reason to begin every sentence with 'I'm sorry'. Obviously if you spill red wine over someone's new shoes, then an apology (along with the offer to pick up the cleaning bill) is necessary. Don't tell people that you're not very good at networking, nor apologize for taking up someone's time. Never apologize for how you look, what you do, or that your name is difficult to pronounce or has an unusual spelling. If you're really finding things difficult, be the one to move on first; don't get left standing there.

Shy people who aren't finding networking easy should take every opportunity they can to strike up conversations with strangers: at the bus stop; in the supermarket queue; at the checkout; with the bank teller. Simply asking 'How's your day been?' is enough. No one is likely to say 'None of your business' unless you're really unlucky. Don't forget that other people are shy too. Regard it as your job to put them at their ease. Pull out all your networking ability and remember that you can make a difference in the lives of other people by smiling, introducing yourself, asking an open-ended question and listening to their answer. Shyness is all about you – and this chapter started by explaining that the art of conversation is all about the other person. If you need further encouragement, remember that introverts and shy people make excellent listeners because they'd rather listen to other people than do the talking themselves. Being a good listener means you are more than halfway to becoming an excellent conversationalist. Now doesn't that make you feel better?

Finally, a word about making elegant exits. If you are to make the most of your networking time, you need to be able to mix and mingle without getting stuck in one conversation with no end in sight. When you are networking you are not expected to talk to people for any great length of time. Even five minutes' conversation with someone should be enough to elicit the information you want, exchange cards and then move on. If you do meet someone you'd like to spend more time with, make an arrangement to follow up later on, before moving on to mix with the rest of the guests.

There are plenty of polite ways to end a conversation and if you know what to say you need not be nervous or embarrassed to do so. One way is to introduce the person you're talking with to someone else, then move on to another group. You could ask for their business card, thank them for it and exit the conversation. Offer to fetch them another drink and as you hand it to them excuse yourself saying that there is someone you need to speak to on the other side of the room. It is perfectly okay to tell someone that you have to meet a colleague who has just arrived, and ask to be excused from the conversation. Whatever you feel comfortable in saying will be fine. Make up one or two lines and practise them before you go to a networking event. As long as you are polite and confident no one will prevent you from ending an exchange. You can do it: exiting is easy once you've got the hang of it; and you need never get stuck in a conversation rut again.

8

Coping with rejection

Be nice to people on your way up because you'll meet 'em on your way down.

Wilson Mizner

This chapter deals with rejection and how to cope with it. No one likes to think they will make mistakes and meet with refusal when making overtures of friendship. Successful networkers are upset when they experience setbacks in terms of reaching their goals and objectives. The distinguishing factor between those who fail and those who do not is, simply, that winners don't give up – ever. They change behaviour, employ new tactics maybe, but they persevere. I have mentioned before that networking is a continuous process. You should never say never. However difficult it is to build a relationship with a prospect, you can achieve success. An understanding of Neuro Linguistic Programming (NLP) could be helpful (see my book, *Understanding NLP*, co-authored with Neilson Kite, and published by Kogan Page). If you find you are up against some complex characters, they will require more time and effort to win round. If at first you don't succeed, don't give up – keep on keeping on. Rejection can be a personal, in-your-face type of refusal. It can also be done in written format – remember the saying 'The pen is mightier than the sword'? So where advice is given on how to cope with rejection, you should bear in mind that you can still be rejected when networking in the virtual community. You could, for example, be banned from a chat room, or if you are messaging people, they could block you. Think about it from their point of view – what could be the reason for their refusal? Is it them, or is it you?

Key point

The most successful individuals who build rich and vibrant networks are those who make an enormous effort to win friends and influence people. They do it everywhere, with everyone, and they do it continuously.

Effective networkers derive satisfaction from every inch of progress they make, however slow it may be. Should rejection occur, they don't despair but renew their endeavours to reverse the process. They may change their approach, and they may have to do this more than once. But they keep on until they turn their failure into a positive outcome. Highly motivated people can do this; less energetic ones don't have that ability. They could certainly do it if they wanted to, but once they've been on the receiving end of a refusal they think that it's pointless; so they give up. They imagine that whatever they do, things will keep going wrong for them. In effect they allow themselves to be drawn into a downward spiral.

To be an effective networker you must be able to cope with negative situations in a positive way. You probably handle rejection to some extent every day in different forms. You arrive at the platform one minute late to find your train just pulling out of the station. What do you do? Probably just wait for the next one. You go to buy your lunch at the sandwich bar and they've sold out of your favourite filling. What are your options? You could choose a different kind of sandwich, or try another sandwich bar. You don't need to burst into tears, take it personally, stamp your feet, tell them you always have that sort of filling and vow never to go into their shop again. This may sound like a flippant example but what does it tell you? It's a matter of attitude, of being proactive in an attempt to turn a negative situation into a positive one. How do you cope when things don't work out as you planned?

Key point

When facing someone's refusal to cooperate with you, think positively. Get over it. Be practical and find another way round the problem.

Sometimes even if you have worked hard to do something – for example, arranging to meet a person at an event with whom you are keen to build a business relationship – things can and will go wrong. You make a huge effort to get to the event on time and your prospect doesn't show. You're so disappointed you flounce out of the event without making any attempt to salvage anything from the rest of the evening. Don't do this; it probably is not about you anyway and was completely out of their hands. Most likely there was a genuine problem – traffic chaos, crisis at work, illness. If you persist in taking it to heart it will affect any future dealings you may have with that person, and this is as unfortunate as it is unfair. The best solution in a situation like this (and everyone faces disappointment in some way on a fairly regular basis) is to send a polite enquiry (by e-mail, telephone or text) to find out what happened: 'Hi Jo, I was hoping to see you at the lecture last night, but you weren't there – hope you're okay.' This will keep the door open to follow up on the missed meeting without loss of face on either side.

A strong positive mental attitude will create more miracles than any wonder drug.

Patricia Neal

Networking isn't always fun. It is a serious business, as it involves opening doors to new business opportunities. Sometimes it's a case of Pandora's Box and you wonder why you bothered. In Greek mythology, Pandora was the keeper of a container holding all the world's ills. She did not know what was inside the box and was ordered never to open it. But the gods had also given her the gift of curiosity, so eventually she opened it. All the world's evils, ills and diseases escaped, but at the very bottom of her box lay one tiny thing: hope.

Should you be faced in a networking context with something going wrong – a point-blank refusal by someone to meet you, for example – it is vital that you suspend any emotional reaction and do nothing until you know the reason for the person's behaviour. You must try to work out why this has occurred if it seems that there is no logic or reason behind it. In a social setting something like this is not helpful; in a business context, if you fly into a rage and behave in an uncontrolled manner, the outcome could be disastrous.

The most common and habitual reaction of someone being rejected is to attack. This reinforces the hurt and makes it more difficult to discover the reason for the rejection. Resolution of the situation becomes almost impossible because of the emotional content. In essence there are two things happening here. There is the act of rejection, which needs to be investigated, and there is the diffusing of the emotions attached to the problem. Remember that someone who delivers what seems like a rejection to your overtures of friendship may be acting on orders, or could have overriding reasons that they cannot divulge to you but which make agreeing to your proposal impossible. A delicate company buy-out or imminent takeover might mean that any networking activity is suspended by senior management until the corporate situation is resolved. Or the executive may be going through a health or marital crisis and will not accept any invitation at the current time. They have sworn their colleagues to secrecy and no reasonable explanation is given for their 'No'. Consider that when you next encounter a negative situation – it will spare you personal hurt and increase the chances of discovering the real reason behind the actions in due course.

Key point

In a situation where the automatic reaction is to defend yourself, pay attention to what is happening; make no assumptions; listen for any free information; ask questions to ensure that the situation is made clear to you. Never ignore the other person's point of view.

If you deal with people in a fair and reasonable way, most situations where a perceived personal rejection has occurred should result in a lowering of the emotional temperature. In a business context, it is essential to take control immediately as part of a damage-limitation exercise. Show interest by dealing politely with the person, let them know you are listening. Ask them to explain their reason for refusing to talk to you. Make sure you understand their objection. Consider the possibility of human error. They may have misheard something about your company, or your role within the organization. They may not have all the facts. Ask them what they want to do, saying that things cannot be left as they are. Offer alternative solutions, not just one. Take responsibility for trying to resolve the issue, or pass it over to the correct person to sort out. Do this at once. If the problem cannot be sorted out immediately, tell them why and explain that it may be a little time before the matter can be cleared up.

Never interrupt your enemy when he is making a mistake.
Napoleon Bonaparte (1761–1821)

When facing rejection, don't take it personally. Commit to overcoming the obstacle as soon as possible without resentment or blame. Don't make promises you can't keep. Neither should you vow vengeance. Getting even won't help. It will only damage still further the possibility of establishing a relationship. This situation hopefully will never happen, but should it do so early on in your networking experiences, reading this advice on handling refusals to cooperate and dealing with rejection may be useful. The advice is equally applicable inside or outside the working environment.

Key point

Despite one of the rules being not to take rejection personally, you might review your own behaviour to see if anything you've done has caused the other party to avoid you. There are some common mistakes that can increase the likelihood of getting a refusal in a networking situation.

Have you been talking so much about yourself that you have put the other person off completely? Could they have said to their staff, 'I never want to attend a business event with that person again'? Remember that you can talk yourself out of a networking opportunity very quickly if you overdo it. Talk about yourself but only very briefly: 30 seconds is about right (see next chapter on the elevator pitch).

Perhaps you are so keen on networking that you've confused it with selling. A lot of people do and it's a big mistake. As soon as you detect a whiff of interest, you leap straight into sales mode – and there's nothing people hate more. The people you want to meet may have heard about your reputation and are busy finding excuses to avoid you. So never confuse networking with selling. Try to use it as an opportunity to establish a good 'match' in case at any time someone should need your services.

Another reason for people refusing your networking overtures may be that somewhere, back down the line, you've failed to give value. Do you remember the important bit about establishing trust? If you let someone down over a deal or failed to keep a promise to someone a while back, you'd be surprised how that sort of thing gets around. Do you lack authenticity or are you seen as not being straightforward? You need to have a reputation as an 'honest broker' if you are going to be accepted and welcomed by others when you network. Reflect for a moment and see if you have slipped up somewhere or with someone, then try to put things right. This could eradicate a negative assumption others might have about you.

Remember, rejection doesn't always come in the form that you might anticipate. Take each occasion separately and try to manage the objection sensitively. Effective networking skills begin with the recognition and appreciation that each person is unique. There are three aptitudes that will help you:

■ Sensory acuity and awareness. The more alert and aware you become to the responses and actions of others, the more you will see, hear and feel.

■ Flexibility. In a situation where you do not get the response you want, you need to be able to change your behaviour until you get your desired outcome. You should not wait for the other person or people to change.

■ Congruence or authenticity. This simply means that what you say and how you say it should convey the same message. Saying sorry is no good unless you mean it.

Key point

By using your communication skills you can defuse negative situations and even turn rejection into an acceptance. You may witness embarrassing situations when you are networking; it is useful to be able to pick up on aggressive, assertive or positive behavioural traits.

Sometimes, when faced with refusal, it seems easier to postpone dealing with the issue. This is because people are afraid of being ignored; afraid of humiliation; afraid of further rejection. But a problem will not go away, it will only get worse if not dealt with. First, acknowledge that there is a problem. If you check your emotions, body sensations and thoughts, you will be in control of yourself. That will assist you in taking control of the issue. Communicate carefully, clearly and positively. If appropriate (and possible) get support from a colleague or a superior. Be flexible in your approach and review your goals: what outcome would be best, realistically what are you likely to achieve? Don't procrastinate; act now to confront the challenge.

When engaging the other party in an attempt to discover the root cause of the problem, pay attention, listen – without interrupting. Show that you can suspend reaction in order to analyse the problem. It is crucial to differentiate between the facts (eg some information may be wrong), assumptions (eg calculations may have been creatively adjusted); generalities (eg perhaps the company is always on the fiddle) and emotions (eg 'How can we trust you now?'). It is unwise to make promises or issue threats, but never view a situation as irreparable.

Case study

Les, a successful accountant, implemented a rebranding exercise in his practice two years ago. Everything changed including the staff. One long-standing client who felt she had a personal relationship with him resented the changes. She was upset that Les hadn't told her of his plans beforehand. For two weeks Les tried to talk to her but she refused his calls. So he wrote to her explaining that despite the company changes, he was still in control and nothing about their working relationship had altered. Following a number of phone calls, she finally accepted his invitation to lunch. The first half was unpleasant while she let rip with a tirade about having been let down, not being informed of the changes in the company and requiring reassurance that it would not affect their relationship. Les listened to her concerns, and accepted responsibility for the way she had been treated. It took another couple of months before she would give him more work. In effect the cost of his rebranding was that it took almost a year to convince her that she could still trust him. Les learned from this experience: he would keep his client in the loop of any company changes in future so that she would not be tempted to move to one of his competitors.

What to do when things go wrong

If you are networking and you come up against some unexpected and unpleasant surprises, here are a few tips which could help. Whatever the situation, remain relaxed if you can. Pause before you react. Rejection can often be deflected with care. But you do need to get to the root cause of the problem. You may not have had the full story from the person who first tells you about it. If the situation is going to need time to deal with, cancel meetings so that you have some spare capacity. Don't add to your problems by failing to turn up somewhere when you are expected. If there are other people involved who could make the situation even more negative, deal with them quickly but firmly.

Success is the ability to go from one failure to another with no loss of enthusiasm.
Sir Winston Churchill (1874–1965)

Relish the unexpected. Rise to the challenge of dealing with a problematic situation. See it as an exciting extension of your role of successful networker. If you are completely stuck, think about someone in your network whom you admire or respect. Ask their advice: what would they do in the circumstances? When you are being 'got at' by someone, it is best to keep your cool. If you can listen without showing any negative or defensive emotions, you will make things easier for yourself.

Key point

Criticism, like rejection, is rarely groundless; but due to heightened emotions, it can often be exaggerated. If you can extract the elements that are useful, they can be turned to positive advantage by acting differently in future to avoid a recurrence of the situation.

Ask those responsible for raising the criticism for their help. By asking their advice and making them part of the solution strategy, you make them less likely to continue to reject you. They could turn out to be influential as a mentor, coach or referrer, if handled correctly. The people who criticize you have not only given you free information but have enabled you to improve your networking and influencing skills. By implementing a solution, you have taken positive steps to improve the future relationship.

This applies whether it is the staff members who have helped you sort out the problem or those who have raised the criticism in the first place. By praising others for what they have done well or contributed, you will reinforce the message that your behaviour is positive under negative circumstances. In networking, the establishment of trust and respect is paramount. Your ability to keep promises is what speaks volumes. Whether it's about keeping to time, returning calls, providing promised information, working to agreed budgets – whatever the reason for the rejection in this instance – you need to correct the behaviour found wanting and then remain consistent in future.

It is when trust wavers that business contacts become shaky. If they cannot rely on your word, you will not be able to rely on them. You cannot make claims about your professional ability if you don't believe them and deliver them. Don't put yourself ahead of your contact's needs. Arrogance, ego and the need to prove yourself right in the face of rejection will work against the situation. Convince your contact that it is for their benefit that you are pursuing the solution to the impasse. When they believe this and accept your efforts to get a resolution, you will gain from the relationship. Remember to be a giver rather than a taker. Transparency is important too: make your objectives clear and understandable.

Different approaches

Many of life's failures are people who did not realize how close they were to success when they gave up.

Thomas A Edison (1847–1931)

Internal networking can be a fraught and troublesome area. Take time to find out who's who in your office hierarchy. Some people are, by virtue of long service rather than high rank, deceptively influential and can easily be overlooked. If you are new to your job, or have recently moved positions to another department, it is well worth spending some time investigating this. In the latter case, you are a new yet old member of staff. Previous relationships and friendships may undergo subtle changes, so take care how you deal with people's feelings. Remember, successful networking is about other people – not *you*. Should there be any resentment among former colleagues that you have won promotion and they perceive themselves as losers, tread carefully. You will find it advantageous if you can discover where you stand. Work out where your colleagues and close teammates are in the 'food chain' and whether they are already supporters. You can also do some detective work to see who may be troublesome when it comes to winning new friends, hearts and minds.

Case study

Anna and Philip are both totally blind. Anna has been blind from birth, and Philip was blinded through an accident in his mid-forties.

Both of them are successful consultants specializing in personnel disputes. They have an unerring ability to make accurate judgements with regard to staff challenges in organizations where they are called in to advise. These two can 'see' more about potential personnel difficulties than a sighted person ever could. They both know this is true because they have developed the use of their 'third eye' – intuition. They pick up on subtle messages that are scarcely visible, and on vocal intonation and physical vibrations.

If you are have recently been rejected by someone you are trying to build a relationship with, step back for a moment and reflect. How did you feel about that person when you first met them? What initial reaction did you get? What did you notice about their voice? Was it warm, welcoming, pleasant to hear? Did they have a firm handshake? Did they smile? Did their smile reach their eyes? What was their scent like? Is their beauty more than skin deep? Suspend your visual senses for a moment and observe with your 'third eye'. Close your eyes, listen to someone's voice, you will pick up on their expression, maybe something indefinable about the set and shape of someone's body if they are walking close to you.

Key point

If you can develop use of the 'third eye' approach, you may reduce the number of times you make incorrect judgements about people or are taken by surprise by their behaviour or actions.

There's no doubt that when you network you will at some time or other have to deal with some awkward people. If you find yourself working with high-maintenance people (who expect everything and give nothing), or downright bullies (the only way they know to communicate is by making someone else feel smaller so that they can appear bigger), a review of your assertiveness techniques may be useful. The key to being assertive is that in any negative situation you leave it feeling okay about yourself and the other person involved. The aim is for a win–win outcome in terms of mutual respect and self-esteem. Also, there will be an absence of anxiety afterwards. You won't have feelings of guilt, embarrassment or frustration.

The difference between being aggressive, passive and assertive is clarified in this way:

An aggressive response is a put-down. It is a personal attack, tinged with sarcasm and arrogance.

A passive response is your choice not to say or do anything confrontational. But it can leave you feeling frustrated afterwards.

An assertive response is a reasonable objection that is delivered in a polite and positive manner.

How do you normally respond to negative situations? If you are going to get the most out of your networking contacts you will need to be able to think on your feet. If you find yourself in a negative situation, an assertive response is one where there is likely to be a win–win. You get nothing out of passive behaviour. You can lose a good deal from behaving aggressively. But what you can gain from being assertive is that you feel good about yourself and the other person. There will be an absence of anxiety and guilt. Once you have worked out what the tangible benefits are, it will make you more assertive in future.

Case study

Your boss asks you to work over the weekend for the second time this month. You know about the importance of the deadline, but it's your son's third birthday and you promised him you'd be home all day and help with his party.

What if you told your boss you've done your fair share already, having given up your previous weekend? You mention that your family life is suffering as a result and it's time he asked someone else. Or you could resign yourself to the fact that working on your son's birthday is inevitable and go home and explain the situation to your partner and child. Then spend the whole of the weekend feeing resentful and guilty. You could say you have other commitments but suggest coming in early on Monday and offer to stay late a couple of evenings that week if that would help.

Case study

You work for a company with an established long-hours culture and it's wearing you out. You decide to cut back to a four-day week and prepare workable solutions to present to your directors.

Your suggestions are turned down, so you plead with the directors, explaining that the way you work is making life impossible. You threaten to resign if they won't compromise.

You could ask for a detailed explanation from them as to why they have rejected your proposal. Once you've seen it, you could rework your proposal to counter their objections.

Case study

In a meeting, a colleague presents one of your ideas as her own. How do you react?

You say nothing because you're worried about causing an argument in front of everyone. But you decide to have a word with her afterwards to set the record straight. You express disbelief and firmly point out that this was your idea in the first place. You say you resent the fact that she's been underhand. Why don't you say how pleased you are that she's backing you up? You invite her to work with you on the project.

Case study

You have an urgent project to complete, so you ask your assistant to help you. He says he has an even more important assignment to complete for another partner so he can't help.

You try to bribe him to fit your work in, but realize that you'll probably have to do it yourself. Try pulling rank and say there's no way this deadline can be missed. He has got to stay late and do the work. Explain about the urgency, that the work has to be finished today. Offer to negotiate on his behalf about the other work he will have to set aside to help you.

Keeping going is more important than winning

How do staff members come across to one another in your organization? Do your staff and colleagues interact easily and with openness? Any anxieties or insecurities will result in rejection of either people or plans and projects. Unhappy people, those who feel threatened or undervalued, will have the greatest likelihood of refusing to enter the culture of relationship building. They will not feel motivated about networking and are more likely to reject others who approach them. People tend to be one of two types: extrovert and introvert. Extroverts are more people-oriented and are likely to buy in to the networking culture. Those who are introverted won't understand it and may reject any attempts to persuade them otherwise. But don't give up on them; once they 'get it' they can become very good networkers. Remember the tip about shy people networking effectively – because they'd rather listen than talk.

If at first you don't succeed, find out if the loser gets anything.
Bill Lyon

A bit of staff bonding goes a long way to enhance goodwill among team members and colleagues and reduce the chances of the difficult characters making trouble for those who enjoy building working relationships.

Key point

Whether you are building business relationships internally or externally, it pays to spend time finding out people's likes and dislikes. A 'thank you' never goes amiss. If praise is due, then say something; and if it can be done appropriately, do so in public. The results can be dynamic.

If looking at ways of building rapport professionally, when it comes to eliminating the chances of rejection, start within your organization first. Seek opportunities to make connections with colleagues on every occasion. This will get them used to the idea that you believe in networking and are highly motivated. It will also convince them that you are likely to continue despite their lack of encouragement. Always keep an eye for openings, whether this is to introduce yourself to new people or include others inside the company in new projects or incentives. An ongoing effort will be required but as you gain in confidence, rejections will decrease or cease to concern you. The more adept you become at making friends and winning people over, the easier you will find it to remove the obstacles placed by those who wish to hold you up.

If you want to win new contacts, work hard to withstand any attempts they make to reject you by misconstruing your communication. Rejection can and will occur when there is a breakdown in signalling. Reluctant networkers frequently attribute the blame to the proactive person. There are a number of ways they can do this: the recipient may not be concentrating; they may have prejudices about the communicator or have made false assumptions about the message. If someone wants to misinterpret your information badly enough, watch out – they will find a way of doing so. Everyone has different ways of thinking, so the idea you want to get across will be subject to different interpretations by others.

Looking at all this, it's surprising that communication doesn't go wrong more often. One study showed that people leaving an hour-long business meeting had, on average, three to four major misconceptions about what had been agreed. Usually you will find that people have a problem admitting that they've hit an internal barrier. So reasons and excuses are then invented for the problem through a process called rationalization. You convince yourself that the fault does not lie with you because that would be too hard to bear. So you rationalize and find reasons why the problem must be coming from the other person.

The critical factor to consider about your attitude as it relates to networking and communication is whether it is positive or negative. Having a positive mental attitude is much more than thinking up witty remarks and the like. It is a way of living in and relating to the world. In this way your attitude controls your life. Attitudes are a secret power working 24 hours a day, for good or bad. It is important that you know how to harness and control them. Success or failure where building relationships with people is concerned is primarily the result of the individual's attitude. Coping with rejection in a positive way is an integral part of this. Remember that a change of attitude can bring about an outstanding change of results.

9

The elevator pitch

Talking and eloquence are not the same thing. To speak and to speak well are two things.

Ben Jonson (1572–1637)

This chapter is about the elevator (or lift) pitch: what it is, how you develop one and how to use it effectively. It is a single sentence that describes your work and which you can deliver in 30 seconds or less – the time it takes an elevator to travel from one floor to another. One memorable lift pitch was overheard at a networking event, and delivered by a smartly dressed guy. On being asked what his job was, he replied: 'I'm in the removals business.' He was actually a surgeon.

If you want to create a compelling elevator pitch, it needs to be short and accurate. Mark Twain said it best: 'I didn't have time to write you a short letter, so I wrote you a long one instead.' If a business person said 'I didn't have time to write a short elevator pitch, so I wrote a long one,' his prospect would probably exit the lift at the next floor. The elevator pitch is about getting your message across in the shortest possible time. When you are on your way to a networking event and you find that you're sharing the lift with someone you've long wanted to meet, that's when you'll need it. If you don't have one prepared, you may never get this chance again. You want to be able to deliver your message before he gets out of the elevator and disappears into that function room. It will be full of other people who will all be trying to get to him before you do.

Key point

It's a well known fact that 'less is more' – but it is so much harder to do.

Do you know why there is so much passion about elevator pitches? It's not just about the end result but about the mental process too. A lift pitch is the purest, distilled essence of your dream and your vision. Developing a lift pitch requires you to articulate what really matters to you, to your organization and to those you want to influence. It forces you to focus. What 10 words best describe your business? See how many different one-liners you can come up with, then choose which one is best. If you were in an elevator one day with somebody you really want to speak to, would you be ready?

How to get your unique message across

Courtois's Rule: If people listened to themselves more often, they'd talk less.

Anonymous

Your elevator pitch belongs firmly in the introductory stages of networking: getting someone interested in you, your business and services. In fishing terms, the lift pitch is bait. Your elevator pitch is for baiting the hook and getting people interested. It should make people want more information, so that before you get out of the elevator, they grab hold of you and say, 'Tell me more.' If they're interested, then you can start feeding them fish. Once they're happily eating the fish, you can close by pulling in the line (or net; depends whether you're fishing for shoals of small fry or for larger species). The elevator pitch baits the hook – you don't need to force-feed them fish. Just get your networking contacts to want more. Get it right and they will ask quite readily.

Key point

The elevator pitch covers *what* (the idea) and the *so what* (tangible benefits). It doesn't include *how* (you are going to do it).

Keep repeating in your head 'So what?' every time you make a statement. That reminds you to include tangible benefits to attract your networking contact. One further important rule to bear in mind with regard to the elevator pitch: always assume short buildings. You may not have 50 storeys in which to explain yourself. The elevator pitch consists of a tag line, a burning problem, an opportunity (reflecting your exclusive expertise or some particular value), a 'So what?' (meaning the benefits for the prospect), a mission statement (which should clarify your tag line) and a call to action. Not bad?

The elevator pitch should change the pulse rate of your listener. In other words, you should be passionate. You don't want 'geek speak' or 'MBA speak'. Speak English and use the *KISS* principle – Keep It Simple, Stupid. If you think about being in the world of horse racing, what would change your pulse rate? The subject might be the racetrack; the specific article is the horse. But what if your lift pitch tells someone this: that you train superb jockeys, that these jockeys win more races than any others and you have the records to prove it. Bait the hook, feed the fish, get them interested. Now wouldn't you say 'Tell me more'?

Key point

If you want to network successfully, your elevator pitch needs to be memorable. You want to be memorable in a positive sense – not a negative one. Sincerity is one of the most influential factors in networking.

No one will be interested in you if you're artificial. If you deliver an elevator pitch it needs to be real too. Being genuine, knowing what you're talking about and meaning what you say may seem elementary but a lot of people (most of whom should know better) make bad mistakes. If you're reporting facts, whether they're about your company policy, a particular area of expertise or specialist knowledge, you must get them right. Should you not be sure about something you'd like to include in your elevator pitch, get someone whose opinion you trust to check it before you open your mouth, otherwise you might regret it.

Use plain language, not jargon or acronyms. You don't want to exclude people, whether members of the general public, newcomers to your network or organization.

After you've spoken, pause. Give people a moment to digest your words and see how they respond to you. If you've got it right, this should be in a positive way. Your lift pitch should get them to the 'Tell me more' stage. Be prepared for this, be ready with all the key information to hand, and let the networking opportunity commence.

A word here about values and branding. People make decisions about others on the basis of both the rational and the emotional. When you are involved in networking and building new business relationships, you will find that these are founded on certain values. Identify those values and make sure your lift pitch includes some reference to them. If your organization's product value underpins everything, your lift pitch will need to engage your listener quickly, emotionally and intellectually. The most powerful concept in marketing is owning a word in a prospective client's mind. For example in motor-industry advertising, certain words belong with the main manufacturers: 'safety' with Volvo, 'driving' with BMW, 'engineering' with Mercedes and 'technology' with Audi. In the fast-food industry, two companies cannot own the same word in a prospect's mind: 'fast' belongs to McDonald's, not Burger King; their word is 'flame-grilled'.

Key point

A good lift pitch will reflect brand identity. The most successful marketing messages must show congruence. Whatever message you want to deliver, it should be accurate, succinct and professional.

Any form of presentation that is scrappy, poorly presented or unprofessional reflects negatively on your organization and the service it offers. By maintaining high standards, personally and organizationally, your lift pitch will reach prospective business contacts in the right way and emphasize your company's identity.

Your reputation directly affects the likelihood of delivering a successful elevator pitch. If you are going to build strong business relationships, you must be motivated, proud of who you are and what you do. Giving out a strong message says as much about the person speaking as the organization to which it relates.

When you get your 30-second opportunity, you want to make the most of it. There are lots of other professionals who will be doing the same thing. Stand above your competitors by making sure your message is irresistible. It should be truthful, sincere, confident, modest and reliable, and it should inspire trust.

What some people say – and what they shouldn't

The human brain starts working the moment you are born and never stops until you stand up to speak in public.

Sir George Jessel (1824–1883)

Some famous people have said some great things, and others have made awful gaffes. Do you recognize any of these famous lines and do you know who said them (though sometimes only supposedly)? The answers follow below. What can you learn from them?

1. I want to be alone.
2. Frankly my dear, I don't give a damn.
3. Come up and see me sometime.
4. Friends, Romans, countrymen, lend me your ears.
5. We are not amused.
6. Let them eat cake.
7. Ich bin ein Berliner.
8. I shall never tell a lie.
9. You cannot be serious.
10. I'm a pretty straight kind of guy.

And who can ever forget this one?

11. I did not have sexual relations with that woman.

Answers: 1. Marlene Dietrich; 2. Rhett Butler in *Gone with the Wind*; 3. Mae West; 4. Mark Antony in Shakespeare's *Julius Caesar*; 5. Queen Victoria; 6. Marie Antoinette; 7. John F Kennedy; 8. George Washington; 9. John McEnroe; 10. Tony Blair; 11. Bill Clinton.

When you are thinking about what to say, and how to say it, you will need to consider the concept of Linguistic Psychology. This is the study of how people interpret what you say. It helps you to adapt your communication style accordingly.

Key point

Applying Linguistic Psychology ensures that verbal communication is (a) understandable, (b) relevant, (c) succinct and (d) memorable.

To explain this a little more: consider the fact that single words or phrases can often have several meanings. If you take, for example, the phrase 'You're coming home with me tonight,' there's more than one way in which this could be construed.

First meaning: imagine you're a weary parent, driving to collecting a teenage son or daughter from a party. It's after midnight when you get there. The noise is deafening. You find your offspring, then they refuse to get in the car, saying they're not coming home because they're going clubbing. You might speak these words in a stern voice and determined fashion, emphasizing the words 'You're', 'home' and 'me'. (Depending on the teenager, this might not do much good, but at least you'd have tried.)

Now try a different scenario. You've been to a social event where you've met a gorgeous member of the opposite sex. Throughout the party the body language has been increasingly encouraging, the conversation flirtatious, including some innuendo. The evening is looking decidedly promising. You utter the words in a – you hope – seductive tone: 'You're coming home with me tonight.' In this instance, all the emphasis is probably on the word 'tonight'.

Third interpretation. You're male and you've been to a business networking event with a number of colleagues. The one you find really hard to like – a female – has been clinging to the drinks table like a limpet and is very much the worse for wear. She sees you getting ready to leave and weaves her way towards you. She explains she's had a little too much to drink and can't drive herself home safely. As she knows you live in her direction, she asks if you could take her home and give her a bed for the night. Your voice is a dry croak as you utter the words, you see your worst nightmare coming true. Your delivery is high-pitched and agonized, conveying sheer and utter horror and disbelief; and this time the words are a question rather than a statement: 'You're coming home with me tonight?' See the difference?

Developing your own message

> *I really didn't say everything I said.*
>
> Yogi Berra

Before you get started thinking up your own show-stopping catchphrase, have a look at the following headlines (found on the internet):

Panda Mating Fails: Vet Takes Over (*That's surely way beyond the call of duty.*)
Miners Refuse to Work after Death (*Sounds perfectly reasonable, doesn't it?*)
Red Tape Holds Up New Bridge (*Wouldn't want to use that firm of engineers.*)
Astronaut Takes Blame for Gas in Spacecraft (*Must be those high-fibre energy bars.*)

Do you see how important it is to check how your message is going to be received?

Crisp articulation of the sentence itself is essential. What does that mean? If someone is described as being articulate, they have the ability to speak fluently and coherently, they are able to pronounce words clearly and distinctly. Once you've crafted the sentence, practice the delivery and some mouth exercises in front of a mirror. If you want to be heard, you need to work your mouth, jaw, tongue and lips. Singers, actors and musicians (brass and wind instrument players in particular) do this before any performance.

There's a great comedy sketch in which Rowan Atkinson plays a prep school master reading the class register. As he calls out the boys' names, articulating carefully, his facial muscles are used to great effect. Try saying the following words with exaggerated mouth movements: Blob, Dollop, Higginbottom, Mole, Mollusc, Plectrum, Pringle, Splot, Zob. If any further work is required on oral agility, you need do no more than go back to basics and find some tongue twisters. Even if you are completely sober, some of these are fiendishly difficult to pronounce. Increase your speed to see how fast you can repeat them without getting into a hopeless tangle:

Cows graze in groves on grass which grows in grooves in groves.
The sixth sheik's sixth sheep's sick.
Six twin-screw cruisers.
A proper cup of coffee in a proper copper coffee pot.
Three tree twigs.
Strange strategic statistics.
Which wristwatches are Swiss wristwatches?

Keep in mind the type of words and phrases you use. They should be easily understood, simple and short, and have positive emphasis. The voice is like an instrument: you must practise using it and rehearse regularly.

Key point

Something actors and professional speakers use is the TBS rule: Think – Breathe – Speak. A relaxed body gives the mind and voice flexibility. Every new thought or sentence needs a new breath.

Before you get going with your elevator pitch, breathe deeply, filling your lungs, hold for a few seconds, then breathe out slowly. This is a great help when you need to overcome nerves. If you want to build up capacity and power, practise counting out loud as you exhale and see what number you can reach.

> *Put yourself on view. This brings your talents to light.*
> Baltasar Gracián y Morales (1601–1658)

Developing your own style is vital. No one can be exactly like another person. Be yourself and get comfortable with rehearsing your elevator statement. When you use it, people will remember you. You don't need to be aggressive or feel you must beat everyone else in the frame. Word of mouth is a powerful device – get your message across well and other people become active ambassadors for you or your company.

Case study

There are two men in the Himalayan jungle. They spot a tiger about 200 metres away and coming towards them. One of the men quickly pulls a pair of running spikes from his bag and starts to put them on. The other looks at him quizzically and scoffs: 'I don't know why you're putting those on, you can't run faster than a tiger.'

'Ah, my friend,' says the man, as he finishes tying his laces, 'I don't need to run faster than the tiger. All I need to do is run faster than you.'

Another way to be memorable is to develop a reputation for giving good recommendations. If you can develop the skill of becoming an excellent referrer it will bring huge rewards. You will never need to pitch for work again and people will be beating a path to your door. Generosity, confidence and motivation are the key skills to being a networker who can provide quality recommendations. If you think being a recommender is your style, then you have a winning networking formula which will work for you time after time. If you offer to recommend your contacts and help them with their business development, they will reciprocate. Based on a successful and memorable lift pitch, which makes you and your company stand out from the crowd, it is possible to win business entirely on referrals with the right network in place.

Ringing the changes and why this matters

> We must believe in luck. For how else can we explain the success of those we don't like?
>
> Jean Cocteau (1889–1963)

If you've perfected your pitch from the foregoing advice, how are you going to cope with pitch decay? Pitch decay is something that networkers must guard against. However effective your elevator pitch is, and let's assume it is good because your prospect has said the words 'Tell me more,' what you say afterwards has to be memorable too. Research shows that only 50 per cent of a presentation is remembered after one hour. Even worse, only 20 per cent will be remembered after just one day. At the end of the week only 10 per cent will have stuck in people's minds.

So what is the 10 per cent that matters? This goes back to the three big points which made up your lift pitch: the tag line, the burning problem and the opportunity (the *so what*). When you're telling your prospect more, as they have requested, emphasize these three points, because the prospect won't remember much else. Some people use the following method when giving presentations: Tell 'em what you're going to tell 'em; tell 'em; then tell 'em what you told 'em. Make sure you identify what your 'must remembers' are and then plan and allow for pitch decay. It doesn't mean there's anything wrong with your elevator pitch, it's simply that people can't remember very much over a long period of time.

Key point

Remember that where an elevator pitch is concerned, less is more. Use it to bait the hook, not force-feed the prospect fish. Keep an eye on your altitude – always assume short buildings. Be passionate and you won't fail.

If you find for some reason that your network isn't as vibrant as it should be, maybe you are stuck in a routine. People change jobs, move on, and if you don't keep increasing your network it will shrink. If you do what you've always done, you'll get what you've always got. People make decisions about where they spend their time based on perceived worth. If the networking events you've been attending have lost their value to you, take a step back and have a look at your options for change.

Maybe you could vary the organizations you belong to, or the ways in which you seek to make new contacts. Make a 'hit list' of new people you want to meet and try to contact between three and five each week. Build in a culture of asking your new contacts to introduce you to one or two new people and do them same for them. This way your 'new blood' simply has to increase.

Speak to people whom you haven't contacted for over a year. Follow up those who have left organizations and moved on to pastures new. Build relationships with their successors and track down your old contacts. They will be flattered you have traced them and be happy to re-establish a connection with you. Who knows, they may just have been waiting for you to contact them. Ask friends and colleagues to invite you to their business networking events as a guest. It's sometimes a good idea to meet a completely new crowd. And what a great morale booster if you get there and someone recognizes you.

You know how to get the most out of the time you invest in networking. You have your elevator pitch at the ready, one that communicates in the shortest possible time what you do in a concise and memorable fashion. It tells people who you are and what type of industry you are in. It explains what you do, how you satisfy a need, achieve a goal or avoid a consequence.

Key point

When breaking new ground, or refreshing your network, give your elevator pitch. Remember the five rules of relationship building: empathy, courtesy, enquiry, interest and respect.

Show empathy. Empathy is the ability to put yourself in the other person's position and see things from their point of view. It may come naturally to you, or you may have to acquire this skill. Empathy has to be visible. Your business contact must feel that you understand. After your lift pitch, set about the task of finding some common ground. It should be possible to establish two or three things in common with a new acquaintance within a minute or two.

Be courteous. Engage with someone by being sympathetic. It will surprise them and make them feel human. Small talk can seem superficial and artificial. Get into real conversation with your networking contact and watch for the warmth of their reaction. Look for visual and verbal clues to assist in establishing the relationship. Make your voice warm and engaging, and use positive body language. Watch for any signs of mirroring to help you.

Make an enquiry. Use open questions to elicit information and encourage conversation. If you're having difficulty in getting information from someone, it can be very frustrating being faced with just 'Yes' and 'No' answers. Remember to ask open questions: ones that cannot be answered by one word. This may be all it takes to get you started.

Show interest. Keep an expression of interest in what you are saying.

Be alert to the possibility of throwing in an unusual question or witty response. Sometimes humour is appropriate to maintain levels of attention. You can ask the other person's opinion about something as a hook for making a comment.

Be respectful. Never assume that your business contact will have the same views and attitudes that you have. The world is full of different people whose ideas, prejudices and opinions may not be similar to your own. Their culture may be different, with some attitudes and customs that seem unusual. In order to build a working relationship, try to understand them. Respect your contact's individuality, and be considerate. Your business contact will appreciate the attitude and respect this shows.

10

Following up

The first step to getting the things you want out of life is this: Decide what you want.

Ben Stein

Networking in the physical world isn't just about meeting people. It has legs. You find new business contacts at networking events, hopefully some seem potentially interesting and open to exploring ideas. If this is the case, you naturally want to take things further. At this stage you begin to look for mutual connections. As you will recall from Chapter 4, Networking in the virtual community, this can be done a lot more quickly online because you can join special-interest groups. In physical terms, however, and in this chapter in particular, the follow-up stage is described. It's an important step in the networking process because this is when you begin making friends with your new business contacts. Refresh in your mind the key networking attributes: curiosity, generosity, confidence and motivation. You ask your new contacts how you can best help them, you are generous with your advice or introductions, you deliver what you promise, thereby creating trust, and you don't stop there. You are motivated to continue, exploring how you can further help each other, which is the underlying purpose of the networking process. This results in solid professional working relationships that can be incredibly rewarding.

Key point

You may not realize it but you've reached the stage where you've actually done a lot of the hard labour, the difficult stuff.

In gardening terms, you've researched the ground, cleared the area, prepared the soil and selected the seeds. Now you are going to plant them. You do need a system or two in place – randomly scattered seeds don't necessarily grow particularly well. A bit of organization and application is all that is necessary. You should, of course, know what you are aiming for (a new job, more clients, market information), in which case your strategy is in place. What is now required is implementation of the follow-up.

Key point

Make sure your network is kept informed of your situation and thank them for their efforts. Never take your contacts for granted. Remember: no contacts = no business.

One of the saddest things in terms of physical networking is when someone makes lots of effort to meet new people and then does nothing further about it. Chances are that you will never see these people again unless you do something. You may want them to remember you and what you do, so that they can refer you to other people. Whatever it is, how can anything happen unless you follow through? After all, you are trying to establish trust. If you collect cards but can't remember what you said or agreed to do, that is worse than not having met anyone in the first place. You'll waste your effort and lose credibility if you don't follow up.

The key to successful networking

If you take networking to be the first stage of the relationship, the follow-up is crucial. You've decided that there is a 'fit' and the relationship is worth taking to the next level. Remember the four attributes needed to be successful when networking: curiosity to start off the networking relationship; generosity to engage the other party; confidence that you can do it well; and motivation to stick to your plan. One of the fundamental rules of networking is to think 'give', not 'get'. Second, be interested rather than interesting. Third, gear your message to other people's needs: successful networking is about them, not you. Physical networking is a lengthy process. Following up does bring rewards – but not quickly. If you're impatient, you should be networking online. You may have seriously underestimated the length of time your physical network will take to mature. Just as you don't often hear of a couple meeting on a blind date, then rushing off to the register office to get hitched the next day (though it is possible), good follow-up develops best when the people involved think carefully about what they are getting into and come to a considered decision.

> *When the character of a man is not clear to you, look at his friends.*
>
> Japanese proverb

What about your oldest friends? Are they also your closest confidants? If the answer is yes, perhaps it's because they have known you for such a long time. Did you grow up together? If so, you'll have lots of things and past experiences in common. Maybe your parents and families were friends before you were born. Were you in the same class at school, spending time together every day for a period of several years? Or perhaps you went through university or college at the same time? In that case you'll have many rich and colourful memories of your student days.

Key point

To get the follow-up process started, identify any common links and themes among the people in your database. You can do it by mind mapping.

On a sheet of paper, start with you, right there, in the middle. Branching out from you, in a number of different directions, are the routes that take you to different groups of people in your life. These include family (everyone you are related to); work internal (the people who work with you: colleagues, boss and staff); work external (the people you meet through work but outside the office: clients, suppliers and others); leisure (those you know from your spare-time activities: at sports or at your favourite bar or club). Next, write the names of no more than 10 people under each group. When you've done that, have a look at the paper and see whether any of these people could be linked together, other than through the one main connection point – which of course is that each of them knows you.

The purpose of being a giver and not a taker in networking is that you build long-term, trusting and respectful relationships. Developing connections with like-minded people is the aim. Why is this? Because if you have an easy and open relationship with someone, they are most likely to know when you need help – as you will, should they require support. One of the best ways to start off is by helping them as and when you can, or by offering your time, skills or talents should the need arise.

Case study

Matt was looking for work. He'd just qualified in landscape-garden design and was trying hard to get a job, looking for advertisements and enquiring at employment agencies. He asked his aunt Rachel, a successful businesswoman with a lot of contacts, whether she could help. Rachel agreed and within a few days had sent an e-mail to a number of her friends and business contacts telling them about Matt. The result: two local companies rang up offering Matt some work experience with their gardening firms. He also landed a couple of small contracts that he was able to undertake as a freelance on a part-time basis for two of his aunt's friends.

Case study

Debbie was about to go off on a gap year. In order to raise some money, she decided to sell her car. She'd been working part-time in the local hospital, so she decided to go back to see her departmental manager to ask if she knew anyone employed there who was looking for an inexpensive car. As Debbie was talking to her boss about this, a group of student doctors were standing near and one of them overheard the conversation. His mate had just been told that his car had failed its MOT so badly that it wasn't worth repairing. As the young man needed transport to get to and from work, it sounded as if this was a possible solution. An introduction was made. The medical student, Steve, didn't want to spend a lot of money but hoped to find something that was reliable. Debbie was happy to accept a realistic price for a quick sale and the transaction was completed.

Setting yourself a monthly target for following up with the contacts on your database is one way of keeping the follow-up process going. If you think it would be helpful, start listing the people you already know whom you'd like to help but haven't been able to yet; those you haven't seen or spoken to in, say, the last three months; and those you still have on your list that you'd like to meet. You never know: someone you already are in contact with may be the link that you need to reach those new prospects. Links and connections between people can be unplanned and spontaneous.

A goal without a plan is just a wish.

Antoine de Saint-Exupéry (1900–1944)

Key point

Once you start using your database on a regular basis to assist your follow-up activity, make sure you keep up to date with any changes of details. Networks are organic and changes occur frequently.

People move house, get new jobs, marry, divorce, produce children, go travelling. In updating, little and often is to be commended, so that it won't become a mammoth task. Ideally, every month is the best plan. This will lessen the risk of you shelving the task because it has become too time consuming. You will probably have sufficient recall that you will remember the meetings or events you attended, have kept the business cards (should you have collected any) or e-mails received if someone wrote to you as a result of making contact. Spending time cleansing and updating your database not only refreshes your memory as to who's who and what's happened (and what hasn't), it also helps you get into the habit of following up and actively working on your relationship-building strategy.

Developing your unique group of contacts

The easiest kind of relationship is with ten thousand people, the hardest is with one.

Joan Baez

Be selective. It's impossible to keep in touch with everyone you meet, and it's not necessary to do so. With the huge growth of networking sites on the internet, the rule of six degrees of separation has probably shrunk to two. (The concept of six degrees of separation emerged from an idea by Hungarian author Frigyes Karinthy and was the basis of research conducted by American social psychologist Stanley Milgram in the 1960s. His 'Small World' experiment, using letters forwarded from person to person, suggested that most people are connected to each other through a chain of about six acquaintances. The 1993 film *Six Degrees of Separation*, starring Donald Sutherland and Will Smith, was inspired by this research.)

The small-world phenomenon is real: the internet has made so much knowledge and scientific research available to everyone with a computer. You can find out how ideas spread, why fashions come and go, how a small failure can cause catastrophic global consequences (whether scientifically or financially). The fact that the 'six degrees' rule has now been overtaken does emphasize that the world is shrinking, everyone can be better connected than ever before, total strangers can, in minutes, have mutual friends, and gossip can spread rapidly.

Key point

Apathy is the biggest threat to your follow-up activity. Keep motivated. If you lose interest, everything falls apart. Physical networking does not survive long if it is neglected.

If indifference prevails, nothing happens. There has to be an incentive to continue to build your network, increase your contacts and develop your personal relationships. This comes down to your own personal attitude. Be active and make sure you attend regular events, receptions, parties, professional interest group workshops, private social functions. Keep up your sport and leisure activities, as they are very useful. But if you join a new club or society, unless you put in some initial effort and turn up to at least three or four events so that your face becomes known and familiar, you will have an uphill struggle to build trust and be taken seriously. There are limitless opportunities to meet people and make good connections, particularly since the internet allows the circulation of information to tens of thousands of people instantaneously. However, persistence and motivation are needed for personal relationships to flourish. Coincidences do occur and it is encouraging when this happens.

> *Do something. If it doesn't work, do something else. No idea is too crazy.*
>
> Jim Hightower (*New York Times*, 9 March 1986)

Case study

A colleague of Dan's invited him to a reception. Unfortunately, on that particular evening, illness prevented her from attending, but she suggested Dan went along anyway. He did what a lot of people dread, and walked into a room full of strangers. The first person who spoke to him when he arrived was (like everyone else in the room) totally unknown to him. To break the ice and start a conversation, Dan asked the man what he did. He introduced himself as William and said he'd retired last year from a career in teaching. Dan enquired where he'd taught and William named a couple of schools, one of which Dan recognized. He told William it was where his elder brother had been educated. He added that his brother still kept in touch with one of his old teachers. William asked Dan if he could remember the teacher's name. Dan told him and William was amazed. That teacher and William had been colleagues for over 25 years and he'd been best man at William's wedding. It is a small world.

To review the networking process and reinforce some of the benefits, remember that networking is the essential first stage. It is the framework or skeleton. It gets you out there and enables you to meet people who can be added to your database of contacts.

Stage two involves making connections: identifying the links and patterns that emerge – mutual friends, connection points such as similar professions, past links such as having attended the same school or university. The final stage, building relationships, has to have a purpose: business, career or social reasons.

In your dealings with other people, the ability to use humour can work wonders. It aids communication, establishes empathy and diffuses awkward situations.

A sense of humour is part of the art of leadership, of getting along with people, of getting things done.
Dwight D Eisenhower (1890–1969)

Studies show that humour has a beneficial effect on people because it raises the immune system's activity and decreases stress hormones.

Key point
When you are following up with new contacts, show them that you have a sense of humour. It can lighten proceedings.

You can often get an impression of whether humour is appreciated by looking around you. If you are in someone's office, for instance, are there any amusing signs, cartoons, slogans or pictures? Do other people seem relaxed and able to joke with each other? If you are with a group of people in a social setting, is the atmosphere jovial and light-hearted? Laughter reduces stress because it is relaxing and calming. It has been shown in hospitals that patients who have had humour therapy recover more quickly from illnesses or surgery than those who do not laugh.

Case study

Claire was attending an important job interview. She was desperate to be successful because it was a position she really wanted. The interviewer was a rather serious man who remarked, when looking at her CV, that her first job had been with the BBC. 'Yes, that's right,' she responded brightly, 'and I've been working my way steadily downwards ever since.' 'In that case, you won't fit in here,' was his swift reply. He had not appreciated her attempt at humour. Needless to say, Claire didn't get the job and learned from the experience that in certain situations using self-deprecating remarks as a humorous gesture doesn't always work.

How to make your network work for you

What if your networking's not working? What do you do then? Are you wondering if you've been wasting valuable time up to now? That's probably not the case but perhaps a quick review might be helpful, just in case there is a minor adjustment or two that needs to be made.

> *A relationship, I think, is like a shark. It has to constantly move forward or it dies. And I think what we've got here is a dead shark.*
> Woody Allen

First of all, remind yourself what networking means to you personally. You probably want to increase your contacts and reach new people and markets, and become better informed. How can you do this? The best way is through others. As you know, it's a lot quicker to network online; the results are almost instant and the numbers you reach can run into thousands. But don't let that laziness factor creep in and deflect you from the importance of making personal contact with others – it can be so much more rewarding. Some obstacles to physical networking involve communication methods. You need to be able to get your message across clearly and professionally, as Chapters 6, 7 and 8 have shown. The 2:1 ratio is something that can't be emphasized enough. You should listen twice as much as you speak (two ears, one mouth: remember and pay attention to the five levels of listening skills). Also, there should be twice as much 'you' in any conversation as 'me'. Networking is all about *other people*. Being memorable is covered in Chapter 9 where I describe the elevator pitch.

Of course, you need to be organized. Big business cannot be won just by small talk alone – although that is important in opening doors initially.

Key point
Successful business networking is a strategic exercise; you'll need a plan, a map, a chart (whatever you want). This will determine who you need to connect with.

Your plan should show how to get to these people; what factors link you together, your shared interests and common aims. Finally, it should indicate what actions you need to take to develop powerful business relationships. Whatever else needs to be done, however you try to exert influence over the relationship-building process, you need to be persuasive in your dealings with your potential clients, influencers and recommenders. You should bear in mind that other people are probably at it as well. If you have researched and found that a particular person is an ideal business contact, it is safe to assume that others will have done the same. Assume that they are as professional as you are. So how do you get to be 'first among equals'? The answer: become a persuader.

If it were just a question of 'heads' or 'tails', and a flip of the coin would decide whether or not you were the winner of a valuable piece of new business, there's not a lot you can do to influence luck. But there are other ways of helping to tip the balance in your favour. How would you define 'persuasive'? A persuasive person is someone who is seen by others as being understandable, attractive and convincing.

Key point

Persuasion techniques involve you being able to communicate to your contact that: they are important and will be treated as such; their opinions and position are respected; they will be dealt with as a unique individual; they will benefit by dealing with you.

Persuasive types are always up front and honest. Make clear to your contact when following up what the facts are; mention any snags there are (and there usually are some); what compromises may be required and how the relationship can work.

To be convincing and effective, your follow-up approach must be individually tailored to the other party involved in the process. (If you do what you've always done, you'll get what you've always got. Be aware of the other person's roadmap and have a flexible strategy.) Say your usual opening gambit is to offer your new contact corporate hospitality at a sporting event. This is not going to influence someone who is more interested in raising money for good causes. They will just regard your gesture as wasteful and unnecessary. You won't have advanced your cause one inch. Each person you are attempting to follow up with will want an approach that recognizes and respects their point of view, matches their personality and interests and so generates a warm response from them.

Bearing this in mind will get you off on the right track. It should quickly show you the reason why the identification and preparation stages are so important. This is complex and there are many things to consider, including your own personal positioning. If handled smoothly, the follow-up will go well. Your contact will know that they are dealing with a professional who takes time and care over the relationship-building process and treats each relationship and contact with respect.

Key point

Communicate clearly, make your words attractive so that your business contact wants to listen and is as keen to develop the relationship as you are. How do you do this? You talk about the benefits.

People do not encourage relationships in business just for friendship. It has to go further than that. They will want a clearly defined purpose. If you explain the reasons why you want to connect with them and that there are advantages to you both, they will understand what's in it for them. The advantages, say, of a small specialist design group collaborating with a large architectural practice means that the small firm can be included in bigger projects than they would normally get involved in. The large company will harness external specialist expertise in an area they do not have covered in-house. Working together to bid for significant projects will result in a win–win solution.

Talking benefits in this way as you describe your ideas for increased working opportunities will support the relationship-building process. It is important to get this right. All networks are different and in some cases you will be persuading more than one person of the advantages of such an alliance. For example, you could be required to influence a board of directors or a group of partners in a professional service firm.

Communicate with everyone, respect their opinion, value their contribution, and gain from the experience. In defining persuasion, it is important to make what you say to your business contact credible. Most people who are experienced in business dealings have a healthy degree of scepticism. They can be forgiven for thinking that you have a vested interest and will be looking for an element of proof. The main form of evidence has to be the persuasiveness of the case put forward, harnessed to the tangible business benefits, followed by proof positive that it can be done.

Let's say you mention the following: 'Two years ago we collaborated with company X who were looking to expand in Europe. Because of our strong associations in France, Germany and Spain, we were able to open up new markets for them in these countries.' This shows your new potential partner that you have a proven track record that backs up any proposal you are making to them. Such compelling evidence would help to convince even the most cynical business contact. There is factual, physical proof here. Your contact can go and check the record and be reassured that what you say is true and not a fabricated claim.

If you find that your claim needs further substantiation, it may be helpful if there are outside elements that can be used. Perhaps your professional association has written a report about the achievements made by you and your previous partner firm. There may be other independent parties who are aware of your successful alliance. Maybe you made a presentation to another organization, or wrote a paper for a professional journal. There are a number of ways in which external proof can be harnessed. These independent authorities are powerful persuasive elements in building credibility with your proposed partner. You can probably think of other examples, applied to your own company or area of expertise. Whatever your profession, industry or sector, if you assemble all possible independent proof factors, you can use them appropriately when required.

Key point

You may be able to strengthen your power to persuade if you have elements of added value that you can bring to the relationship-building process. This will depend very much on your individual expertise or company policy.

However, where possible, if you can offer more than usual, more than the competition, more than expected, then this could have irresistible appeal to your business contact. A successful insurance company clearly took this on board when choosing their company name: More Than. Any such device can act in a number of different ways: to help you get a better hearing; to help improve the weight of the case you can present; to help persuade people to act now rather than later.

A simple way to progress your persuasion strategy when following up is to drop someone a line after making a new contact. An e-mail, a letter or a hand-written note can be sent to let them know you enjoyed meeting them. Try to point out something specific that you talked about, so that it will help jog their memory as to who you are. Some people meet a lot of new faces every day and might struggle to remember you. Simply referring to the fact that you'd both recently been on holiday in Italy could be enough.

In some cases the most effective method of follow-up is a personal note. The reason why this is worth doing is that not a lot of people bother with handwritten communication because it's a lot easier to send someone an e-mail or a text, or call them on their mobile. A polite note, written on decent paper or card, with a good pen and legible handwriting is a sure-fire winner every time. Impressions count, don't they? There's just something rather cheering about seeing a good-quality envelope sitting on your doormat or on your desk.

Take care with wording and expressions, because the recipient cannot see you or hear you. The reader has no option but to accept what they read and if it is at all ambiguous it is liable to be misinterpreted. With a personal thank-you note, use your contact's business address, because it is, after all, a business relationship. You may be thanking them for inviting you to a social occasion but keep the message simple and easy to read. Layout is important. Avoid innuendo, sarcasm and doubles entendres.

If you don't have time, can't find any paper, don't possess a decent pen, then a word-processed letter is fine to send to your contact. It's far better than no follow-up at all. It's the thought that counts and 'thank you' are very important words.

Should you feel that e-mail is more appropriate, check which address is best. Your contact may have more than one. There may be confidentiality issues, particularly if your exchanges have anything to do with career progression or delicate business negotiations. If you decide to use the contact's company e-mail address, be circumspect. E-mails may not always reach their recipient directly. Some people have staff who scan e-mails before forwarding on to the main addressee. If your e-mail is likely to be read by someone else, be extra careful. No references to personal habits – theirs, yours, other people's; it's just too risky. On a more practical level, keep e-mails short and to the point.

Whatever method you use doesn't matter – as long as you do something. If you promised them some information, always follow through. Aim to send any materials within a week of your meeting. Other points include: if you see them mentioned in the media or in a magazine, do mention that to them. If there's nothing else you can do, just invite them for a catch-up drink or coffee. Despite busy schedules, it is always good to have some excuse to take a bit of time out. Most people appreciate a chance to interact with someone over a free drink.

11

Sharing information and contacts

A wise man will make more opportunities than he finds.

Sir Francis Bacon (1561–1626)

This chapter contains advice on sharing information and contacts. Why should you, after all your hard work up to now, want to do this? Surely the contacts you've collected so far should be kept to yourself, so that you can get as much as possible from the connections? But you are a successful networker, and you know that building quality business relationships is all about giving in order to receive. So sharing information and contacts is part of the process, not something you should regard as a loss or 'give-away'. Being generous to others is something you actually want to do because you know the value of putting other people first. It is the best way of ensuring a steady flow of recommendations coming back to you. Whether you are networking online and doing all this via e-mail, chat room, forum, or Twitter, or doing it physically, in face-to-face meetings, it makes no difference. The results are the same: be generous and wait, the rewards will come to you. It's like winning a prize when someone offers you a referral. It is usually an introduction to someone you would have been unlikely to meet without their intervention. Referrals are often given (or received) for a number of different reasons: being professional, prompt and price conscious will always drive referrals from others. They should also drive the referrals you are giving too. The more proactive you are, and if you keep your visibility high, the more you should be able to effect excellent referrals for others; and they will respond in kind.

If you've been paying attention so far, you will have an idea from all of the people you're in contact with which will be the best sources of referrals for you. Take, for example, people who sell insurance, offer architectural and building services: they know that estate agents and surveyors are good referral sources for them. The former groups have services that are needed by people who own houses. The latter groups act for people who are, or are about to be, home owners. There is rich potential here for cross-referral. Research, generate information, possible leads and introductions to other influencers that you think would be of interest to those contacts you most want to help. If you can, think out of the box too; there are the not-so-obvious connections that also pay dividends. In other words, don't preselect your contact sharing too rigidly. Take a moment to list the potential sources of referrals you have for those in your network. Then have a look at who among your contacts might be interested in receiving such introductions. All you need then is to make a plan for bringing the two contacts together.

Developing a close contact network of referral partners can be done formally or informally. It needs to work both ways: connecting people to help their businesses develop, and their returning the favour to you. It is particularly helpful if you are new to networking or are running your own company. It helps you get over the ground quicker. Developing referral partners can make all the difference to your networking success. One thing is certain: the more generous you are, the more you will receive in return.

Being generous brings rewards

Personality can open doors, but only character can keep them open.
Elmer G Letterman

Why do recommendations and referrals work? Because recommendations come from a trusted source – someone else who has had personal experience of the individual or of the company's service or product. Usually the recommender has no vested interest in the business, so it's not a case of pressure being exerted or commission being generated. The best sort of recommendation is independent and unsolicited. In business terms there's a rapid conversion rate – acceptance is dramatically accelerated because the service or product is not being 'sold'. This is what makes referrals the perfect mechanism for rewards. You are allowing people to 'buy', not trying to 'sell' them something.

First, look at referrals for other people's benefit. When you practise being a recommender, start with something you are sure of: for instance, one of your own suppliers. Are they professional, competitive – in terms of price – and do they deliver what they promise? This could, for example, be a firm of carpet fitters who are prepared to work after hours, evenings or weekends, to lessen disruption to someone's business. Ask your new contacts how you can help them. If they mention something that you can respond to, introduce them to companies you've worked with or whose products or services you've experienced and trust. This will work in your favour.

Key point

You should make it a rule when cultivating a business relationship to ask how you can assist. Don't sell yourself, your products or services; offer to look for referrals for them.

What organizations or people do you know whose services and products could benefit your new contact? Check your information; make sure you have the correct contact details of the company you wish to recommend. It is your responsibility as the recommender to pass this recommendation on in a professional way. Saying casually, 'Oh, I think their website is "compareamarket.com"' when in fact it's 'comparethemarket.com' isn't good enough.

Receiving referrals comes as a result of the referrals you've offered to others. Referrals that you are offered are the rewards for having built up a reputation for generosity. You created your network, made your connections, developed a relationship with people and now it's all coming together. Like a harvest, the rewards only appear if the conditions are favourable (ie deserved).

Key point

Referrals are the most powerful and lowest-cost way of building or developing your career or business. They do take time to achieve, so don't be impatient. They are best if they're built on secure foundations.

You can ask for a referral if you're confident enough to do so. A good time to do so is when you've introduced someone to one of your contacts who subsequently awards them a project. Or you may have successfully completed a couple of pieces of work for a client; ask them if they would refer other people to you if they're happy with your services. Should you have solved a problem for someone, they might be glad to reciprocate in some way. Giving a referral is a way of saying thank you when you've been helped.

If you are leaving referrals to chance, and thinking of them only as an occasional welcome surprise, you are ignoring an essential part of your networking strategy. Someone who knows that you and your company are genuine, and is prepared to pass that information on to an interested third party, is worth cultivating.

Referrals are about relationships, respect and trust. Successful networking is about developing quality relationships with others. Collaborative relationships are necessary if your networking is going to yield profitable results.

New business obtained on the recommendation of other people is highly profitable; such clients usually spend more and are loyal. But few companies actively seek referrals. The 19th-century Italian mathematician, Pareto, gave his name to Pareto's Law. It is sometimes known as the 80/20 rule. It suggests that 80 per cent of your business comes from about 20 per cent of your clients. A recent survey showed that almost 80 per cent of a company's customers would be willing to act as referrers for them. Unfortunately, directors and managers only usually approach about 20 per cent of their client base for referrals. A company that asks for referrals from 80 per cent of its existing clients could increase its annual turnover by 20 per cent.

Key point

The success of your networking equates to how much you know about other people, their needs and objectives. Find out as much about your contacts as possible; you'll find it's a lot easier then to offer them the right introductions.

Applying the same principle in another way: it costs a quarter of the amount to retain an existing client than it does to win a new one. If you can keep your clients happy, they will refer business to you. You can continually extend your network by means of enquiring and listening. Feedback is always useful. Anyone can ask for feedback from clients, contacts and influencers. Among other things, it will tell you: who your best clients are; whether your contacts are likely to become your clients; why a person is your client and not someone else's; what they want; how they feel; what they think; what sort of initiatives they would appreciate;

what you can do to encourage loyalty; how you can give yourself a competitive edge over other companies similar to yours.

All the above suggestions add up to one thing: asking for feedback makes your contacts feel *valued.* If you take the time to ask people's advice, they will be flattered and feel that their opinions matter. Many successful networkers use this on a personal basis (as a means of touching base with their contacts and checking on the temperature of their relationship); companies use this method to enhance corporate connections and reinforce existing business relationships. You don't have to ask all these questions in a formal 'survey', though that's how some organizations do it and it works for them. You could simply drop one or two enquiries into a friendly phone call or e-mail or the next time you happen to be contacting someone. But you should remember that there are many different ways of showing curiosity – one of the core attributes for successful networking. If you don't know what's happening with your contacts, and how they feel (about you, your company or anything else) you won't recognize referral opportunities when they occur, or how to make the best of them.

Don't over-promise or under-deliver

> *If you make it plain you like people, it's hard for them to resist liking you back.*
>
> Lois McMaster Bujold (*Diplomatic Immunity*)

Apart from being a recommender to others, there's another aspect to successful networking and keeping your contacts happy: becoming an influencer. Influencing skills, like referral skills, work both ways too.

Key point

Influencers are people who can affect (indirectly) the way someone thinks or acts. In a networking context, this approach is used time and time again by those who like to make things happen but from a distance.

It is unwise to pretend you are in an influential position if you aren't. Making promises you can't keep is not clever, and someone will appear sooner or later to put the record straight. On the other hand, you may be more influential than you realize. Don't assume that influential people are only the ones who hold high office. If you have a wide range of contacts, you will find some people who are not in powerful positions of seniority can wield considerable power.

Case study

The board of directors of a company decided, as part of their modernization strategy, to make their two buildings interconnect (they were separated from each other by a busy road). They commissioned architects and consultants and applied to the local planning department, because they wished to erect a bridge to link their two structures. A number of applications were made but all were refused. The directors spent many hours and much money researching other solutions but came up with none. One morning the chairman of the board was driving to work, and saw ahead of him the caretaker on the other side of the road. The man disappeared into the building but by the time the chairman passed that spot he saw to his amazement the caretaker standing on the other side of the road. He stopped the car, shouted to the caretaker, 'How did you do that? Get from one side of the road to the other without walking across?' The caretaker told him there was an underground maintenance passage which was known to a few members of the workforce. For some reason it had not been put on the site plans.

(from *Making Management Simple*, published by How To Books)

Case study

Tom worked for an international corporation that was hierarchical in its approach. One day he urgently needed the advice of the finance director on a particular matter. He went through the usual channels and asked the FD's personal assistant if he could possibly see him for 10 minutes. She replied that he was not available for two weeks. Tom knew the decision couldn't wait that long, so he went to find the finance director's driver, George. He asked George if he knew where the FD was. George told him to be at the main entrance at 3.00 pm that afternoon, as he was taking him to the airport. Tom was waiting by the door as suggested at the appointed time. The FD spoke to him, told him to get in the car to ride with him to the airport. They were able to discuss the issue in private, advice was given by the FD and Tom's dilemma was solved.

(from *Making Management Simple*, published by How To Books)

People at any level can become influencers. Whether you're starting off in your career, have been working for a number of years, or are about to retire, you're probably in a position to be an influencer yourself. This could be because of the people you used to know, or currently know, or the experiences you have had along the way. To be an effective influencer, cultivate relationships upwards, downwards, internally and externally – from chairmen to car park attendants. Have you ever wasted hours in a busy day searching for a colleague or member of staff? If you're under pressure and they are being particularly elusive, ask the receptionist whether the person you're looking for has been seen coming in or going out. Thinking creatively can solve problems; the right piece of information, however small, can make a huge amount of difference.

Key point

Maintaining a valuable personal network doesn't mean just getting to know the great and the good. It pays dividends to get to know everyone in your personal network and discover their individual strengths.

Some of the most influential people in your network could be the hard-working, non-political types, who are great resources of information and advice. Outside the workplace they could be the people who've lived in your street for decades and know every detail about the local area, who's who and where they live. At work they are the ones who know the inside and outside of the organization, their department and most of the personnel. In your social life, in your club or association, these people have been members for years and have background information on all the officers and members past and present. What rich sources of influence such people are. Why not ask their advice; many people overlook them on the basis that they aren't high flyers. Far better to be on good terms with them and tap into their knowledge than find them saying afterwards, 'If only you'd asked me, I could have told you...'

Try to develop your own influencing skills. There is probably more than one area where your specific knowledge could have an influence on something one of your contacts wants. The more you look for opportunities to be an influence for good, the easier it becomes. You should put as much emphasis on doing it internally (for colleagues, staff and superiors) as for your external contacts.

Just as was mentioned earlier, to keep an existing client happy costs a quarter of the amount of getting a new one; if you think how costly it is for companies who regularly have to replace staff, keeping the good ones makes sound business sense. When a key member of staff leaves a company, the organization is often unaware that it would have been much cheaper to tackle the issues that made the person quit than go through the expensive steps needed to replace them. The real impact on businesses that lose staff regularly and are constantly having to recruit new ones is that it probably takes a year's salary to arrive at break-even point, the point at which the new member of staff turns from being a net cost to adding value.

Could there be a way in which you could influence someone from not leaving their job, if you knew they were thinking of quitting? It might be a matter of helping them directly by means of mentoring them. It could be that your influencing skills are used indirectly, such as saying to a senior manager how concerned you are about a colleague who seems to be under stress. From a company point of view, anyone unhappy at work has low morale, is absent more frequently. If they have staff reporting to them, these people would be demotivated and the department's productivity would drop. Perhaps you could make a difference in some way. When looking at ways of being an influencer, be aware that your influence could act for an individual or an organization.

People make an enormous difference to any organization. What motivates and drives them to release their potential is the way they are treated by their company. Firms need to find creative ways of motivating employees, sharing knowledge with them for the benefit of the whole organization. It could be an environmental issue – such as the provision of a pleasant café area for informal meetings, or the colour scheme and furnishings of the office area. It could be a change in the managerial and organizational culture. What about a different dress code – something more informal if the company has a predominantly young staff? Flexible working patterns would be popular if a number of the staff have young children. You may be in a position to influence something or someone. What it takes is the ability to think creatively for the benefit of others.

Honesty is always the best policy

Friendship is constant in all other things, save in the office and affairs of love.

William Shakespeare (*Much Ado About Nothing*)

To network successfully, you need to interact with all types of people. Some will be extrovert, others introvert. Some are highly people-aware, love going out and about. Others shy away from personal relationships, and are more task-oriented. If you recognize that someone doesn't do face-to-face stuff very readily, don't ignore them or write them off. Such people may be difficult to deal with interpersonally, but perhaps they would be perfectly happy as part of your online network. The point being made here is that sharing information and contacts can be done with everyone, but not necessarily using the same method. The trick is to find the best way of doing it for the greatest effect. If you really hate going to networking events to meet new people, don't keep forcing yourself to do it. You probably won't do it particularly well, so you might as well save yourself the agony and the effort. On the other hand, you might happily stay up all night sending electronic messages, blogging or tweeting. Don't beat yourself up – play to your strengths. If you feel a certain part of the networking process isn't for you, there is usually more than one way of getting from A to B. Honesty is the best policy.

Case study

Elena had just landed a new job. She was excited and showed great enthusiasm. Her boss asked her to accompany him to a business meeting in Scotland, flying in the company plane, so that he could check whether she could handle responsibility. At the airport Elena seemed nervous. Her boss thought it was the prospect of meeting so many important people while being relatively inexperienced. About a minute into the flight, Elena leaned forward and was sick all over her boss. It was a disaster. The situation was rescued only by some quick thinking on the part of the cabin crew – they arranged for some new clothes to be available at the destination airport for both Elena and her boss. The meeting went well and, to her surprise, Elena didn't get the sack. Her boss did insist that she travel by train where possible in future. If only Elena had been honest with her boss about her air sickness, she could have saved herself a mortifying experience early on in her career.

You can't get out of situations just by saying 'There – I tried it and it doesn't work.' You just have to persevere a bit; that's what counts. Neither can you do nothing and expect to get results. People can change (a bit) but someone who is of a quiet disposition and is a great listener is not likely (as a result of reading this book) to become the most talkative and lively person at every networking event in future. You should be open-minded and have a go at learning new techniques and habits. Some habits have the power to alter your outlook on life. If you know yourself and your limitations, it's only common sense to play to your strengths and not worry unduly about your weaknesses.

Regard networking as requiring a light touch. When you have to deal with introverts, take the networking process very slowly. It cannot be conducted at anything like the speed that those who are more relaxed can handle. Offer reticent people the opportunity to contact you online rather than insisting on them accompanying you to every event you can think of (they would probably make an excuse and not turn up anyway). However, they might well be happy to become part of your virtual network, and – more important – introduce you to theirs. Keep in mind that if it's okay for them, it's okay for you. There is never just one way of doing something – in networking you are spoiled for choice.

Key point

It is important to pick up on other people's strengths, and be honest about your own. Have a think about the following: how much do you really know about your contacts; do you ever consider what their favourite way of networking is; which group activity they most enjoy; whether they fall clearly into one of the following categories: decision maker, mover and shaker, influential persuader?

You know that each of your contacts is valuable. Work with them in a way that allows them to shine. It takes a lot of effort to fit a square peg into a round hole and while you're struggling, some of these valuable contacts will get lost or the relationship damaged. Some people may be influential but only on an occasional basis. Just because someone doesn't want to keep in contact with you on a daily, weekly or monthly basis doesn't mean you should ignore them. Contacting them once a year could be just right for them. Update them with current news about mutual friends, family, work – if nothing else, getting a bit of information from them about what they're doing now and what's going on in their network will most likely be useful. You can keep in contact with people by whatever means is most comfortable for them. Remember: networking is all about others, not what's easiest for you.

Whatever you do, whether you are building relationships socially, in the workplace, online or face to face, it pays to think about other people's perspectives. Remember that their map of the world is different to yours. Be honest, be flexible and by changing your approach you will get the best results. (See also *Understanding NLP* by Neilson Kite and Frances Kay, published by Kogan Page.)

Finally, think of where and how you might put these suggestions into practice. You should be open to new opportunities to make connections with your network. Don't have a rigid framework for building relationships. Better to be flexible than outstanding. If you can make other people feel at ease, you will develop a reputation for being influential. As mentioned earlier, presentation counts. Whether that is physical or written, keep an eye on different ways to make people feel relaxed as part of your network. An ongoing effort will be required from your end, but the possibilities are endless. If you are generous with your time and talents for other people's benefit, but honest with yourself as to how you can best do this, making lasting and valuable friendships is easy.

12

Managing and growing your network

I was always looking outside myself for strength and confidence, but it comes from within. It is there all the time.

Anna Freud

So now you've covered the subject of successful networking, where can it go from here? The short answer is: wherever you want. But you must have a strategy and know what you want to achieve.

Regard this chapter more as a review than breaking new ground. To recap: no network is perfect; there are always gaps that need filling and there is always work to be done. But that's one of the advantages. A network is organic – like a living language. Take, for example, English: every time a new edition of the Oxford English Dictionary is published, there are numerous updates to look out for. These include new words, new meanings for old words and adopted words which have come in from other languages and cultures driven by sociological and demographic changes. Your network should reflect the same features: it should constantly evolve, change, develop and grow. From the preceding chapters you should have enough advice on how to construct the best possible network for you. From here you should be able to decide the best direction for it to take. It should never cease moving, otherwise it will stagnate. The last thing you want on your hands, as we saw Woody Allen observe in Chapter 10, is a dead shark.

Your original plan might have been, say, as a small business owner, to become so well connected that you need never have to pitch for work again. In which case, your network should by now be stuffed full of contacts from innumerable companies, micro- to mega-sized organizations, located in all parts of the globe. The common link would be that all of them, at some time or other, could use your services. This would ensure there was no risk of the feast-or-famine cycle familiar to so many entrepreneurs. You might have a strategy that involves making the right contacts and being well connected in a niche area, so that you can rise to the top of your chosen profession ahead of your equally well-qualified, but less widely connected, colleagues or competitors. This network may be in place right now, but your main pre-occupation from here on in is to track changes. This would involve you keeping your ear to the ground to check where those who can 'put in a word' (the influential decision makers, movers and shakers and recommenders) can be found at any given time.

Plans are only good intentions unless they immediately degenerate into hard work.

Peter Drucker (1909–2005)

Key point

In case you haven't quite got your network to where you feel it should be, remember that it takes time to grow a network and it will never be still. There is always a number of outside factors that affect it – not just your own actions.

Outside factors include other parties' positioning in a decision-making process; the success or failure of rivals of yours who may be hunting the same prey. As long as you remember that your networking strategy should retain the same objectives but the process of reaching them is sometimes subject to change, you need not worry. Remind yourself that curiosity, generosity, confidence and motivation will get you there, but that it will take time to achieve your goal.

Even when circumstances force you to deviate from the planned route, you should keep your strategy firmly in mind and get back on track as soon as you can. You will need to use different tactics, as well as playing to your own unique strengths, to move the process along. Try to keep in mind the importance of seeing things from 'the other side's point of view'. Learn something at every stage – even if it's how not to do it in future.

Continuing your success

Key point

Keeping going requires you to continually apply the four key attributes of networking: curiosity (the ability to ask for things in an appropriate way and in a timely manner); generosity (knowing when and what to give to people within your network); confidence (being able to show by example that you are worthy of respect and inspire trust); and motivation (the most important factor of all; the purpose behind your endeavours that gives you the ability to keep on going, and going, and going...)

Think of it as a cycle, because that is what successful networking is: the constant checking, updating, increasing and achieving of new connections. Now that's exciting.

In terms of results, while pursuing your goal (the perfect network for you), does money or profit matter? How do success and the acquisition of wealth relate to the give and take of networking? To what extent should you try to win prizes, earn rewards or acquire large sums of money? And will doing so help you to get better personal connections and be a more successful individual? While on this subject, here's another difficult question. Is it possible for you to be truly happy whether you're rich or poor? Have you ever thought about it? Surely it is much easier to be happy if you're rich? You must know some people who are both poor and unhappy. But there are a number of seriously wealthy people who aren't very happy either. They may live very comfortably in their palatial homes, surrounded by every available luxury. But despite this, they can be as miserable as the poorest people on earth and living a fairly isolated existence.

You could quite wrongly assume that the acquisition of money is a cure-all for your problems. You could also think that by being a successful networker you're bound to achieve riches and greatness. Having deep pockets can solve a number of problems – it takes some of the discomfort out of life, for sure. But networking for profit isn't the only goal you should have in mind. The chances are that those who think money is everything, and are driven by financial incentives, consider themselves great networkers. They may have enough financial clout to develop a huge network, and may be driven by this urge to acquire more wealth, and higher rank, but how much goodwill are they likely to generate? Do people like them for themselves or just for the power of their chequebook? Buying your way into networks isn't what it's about. Such ruthless and aggressive characters seem to get where they want to be by riding roughshod over everyone else. Not much 'giving to receive' visible on their map of the world. Sadly they don't realize that what they are doing isn't real networking.

Key points

If you are looking at networking as a means of achieving a healthy, secure and balanced life, you should concentrate on the pursuit of happiness, not the acquisition of money.

Provided you tend your network and keep it healthy, your investment is secure, whatever happens to the global economy.

Do you have an action plan regarding increasing your contacts?

Do you regularly review your business relationship strategy? Do you actively develop your rapport-building techniques, establish targets and measure results? Have you conducted any feedback enquiries recently, and if so, what information did they reveal? Did you make any use of it?

There should be something here to keep you busy for a while. If you want further things to do, have a look at the following checks and balances. As you know, the amount of information you can gain from your contacts is massive. Do you take advantage of this? Why not, for example, review the five most recent exchanges you've had. It doesn't matter whether these are e-mails, chat rooms, blogs, face-to-face meetings, telephone calls or letters you've received. What did you learn from them? What notes did you make at the end of your encounter? Did you ask yourself why the other party said what they did? Was it something that you agreed with, disagreed with, or did it leave you feeling that they'd misunderstood something you'd said?

Try to get into the habit of mentally reviewing every exchange after it's finished. If you can analyse the results unemotionally, it should help you improve your relationship building next time. There's no such thing as the 'perfect exchange', so every interaction (physical and virtual) could be improved. By adjusting the way you communicate with your contacts you will avoid repeating your mistakes. Don't confine yourself to critiquing after an exchange; effective planning is another way to get more out of any situation. The difference between being prepared and going in unrehearsed could be just a matter of a few minutes of your time, thinking things through (a short mental agenda) before you pick up the phone, dash off an e-mail or start a meeting.

Remember that well-known mnemonic, applicable to so many activities. When you are trying to develop your personal network, remember to work SMART. This involves:

Specific: be clear about what you want to achieve.
Measurable: identify the stages so that you can track progress.
Achievable: can you really do it? Be honest. Don't be over-ambitious.
Realistic: should you start the relationship-building process now?
Timed: work out when you expect to meet your objectives. In weeks, months or years?

Bite off more than you can chew, then chew it. Plan more than you can do, then do it.

Anonymous

So how do you balance nurturing existing relationships with finding new ones (which will then need to be nurtured along with the others)? It is a constant dilemma for anyone who wishes to progress. Some people have great difficulty finding time to devote to networking in addition to other work priorities. To do justice to the importance of it, you may find that a systematic and consistent approach helps. What you are trying to avoid here is a feast-or-famine scenario in your networking strategy: either doing lots of networking or not enough. If you nurture your contacts, you should not have to spend a lot of time contacting people you don't know, at least not on a regular basis. All your connections – even the newest you are following – should be able to generate warm leads because you should be able to mention a name to someone who has referred you, or recommended you contact them.

Key point

Whether you are using your network to look for work, find information, research ideas or socialize, using one personal contact to lead to another is a great way to increase your sphere of influence.

You should always check whether you can mention your existing contact's name when speaking to a new one. Provided you offer them something in return, they will most likely be generous in agreeing to this request. Ask them if there is anyone among your contacts that it would be useful for them to meet, and make a point of following up on a request.

If you are searching for ways to grow your business, seeking new ideas and exploring concepts that will leverage your brilliance, don't overlook your competition. Shifting your focus to view the competition as a resource rather than a rival allows you to discover opportunities that would otherwise remain unknown to you. Thinking of competitors as allies rather than rivals is not really new. Strategic alliances are often the way forward for small-to-medium-sized firms. Cooperation with competitors, customers, suppliers and companies producing complementary products can expand markets and lead to the formation of new business relationships and, in extreme cases, create new forms of enterprise.

Key point

In networking terms, cooperation makes more sense than competition. The idea of teaming up with competitors to develop new ideas and to make your company better at what it does delivers a challenge to many people.

Strategic alliances can be formal and encompass only a specific project. At other times they are for information and are active with only certain types of projects. If your company is client focused, you will actively seek out the best ideas and ways of serving your clients' needs. Combining strengths can produce amazing results. By collaborating with a competitor you might be able to win new contracts that neither of you could secure alone. One plus one can often equal much more than two. Consider having at least three people or companies in your database to whom you would refer business without hesitation. There may be a mutual understanding that the favour will be returned. Whether you have arranged a referral fee, a reciprocal referral, or you are the one that wins the project, everyone is a winner.

It is essential to know the best firms producing the complementary or related services in your own market. Knowledge is power and if your clients perceive you as the place to go for information, your business reputation will grow. Your clients will value your knowledge and connections in the market. You can learn something from everyone and every situation. No one can possibly have all the answers, and that is why sharing best practice is so important.

Key point

Sharing best practice does not mean sharing trade secrets or colluding on fees. It means coming together for improvement. True professionals subscribe to the principle of abundance and see the power of helping each other to get better: 'A rising tide lifts all boats.'

However, do bear in mind the possible pitfalls when contemplating strategic alliances with a competitor or anyone else. One possible issue is the lack of common goals among the parties. If the collaboration does not work, perhaps the synergies were not real or the communication system was flawed. It is wise to do some research before committing yourself to such an alliance –

a corporate version of the pre-nuptial agreement? The obvious benefits of strategic alliances mostly outweigh the risks. It is important to pay attention to whether you really can work together. Complementary areas of expertise are one thing, but do the personality types fit together? The question to ask is 'Can they really add value to the project?'

Creating successful strategic alliances is a valuable skill to acquire. You need to have complete awareness of your own strengths and weaknesses, as well as those of your company. Look for complementary strengths in your competitor-cum-ally. Ideally they will be someone who actually makes you look better at what you do. Always be open-minded to new opportunities and collaborations. You could seek out movers and shakers in your industry or profession. They would regard it as an innovative way to progress and it is another potentially valuable way of harnessing the power of successful business relationships. If you keep your mind open and alive to other ways of increasing the scope of your network, you are almost certain to find plenty.

Uncovering new ground and reaching new heights

So what else is there that you can do if you are determined to continue onwards and upwards? What should you do to ensure you discover new ground and reach for the sky? You may be able to create networking opportunities by being observant. This sounds obvious but is often easily overlooked. Scan the internet, websites, social networking sites, other media, press, TV, professional journals etc to see what names appear. If you've recently read something about one of your personal contacts, get in touch with them and say where they were mentioned, and how pleased you were to see it. You can bet they will be flattered and remember that you took the time to call them. By being observant and showing them that you take an interest in your contacts, you will ensure that they will remember you.

Maybe someone you know has just moved into new premises across the road or launched a new website that is rather good. If they are on your contacts list, make a point of contacting them to touch base. Anything you can do to establish yourself in someone's mind will be helpful when trying to develop your business relationship or personal network. You never know when a chance encounter will provide a connection. It doesn't always lead directly to work, but more often than not it will have a positive effect in some way or other. It could be as simple as being able to remark to one of your personal contacts, 'I didn't know X was a friend of yours. I've just been talking to him.'

Key point

Gone are the days when you could make contact with people only during working hours. Thanks to the internet being available everywhere, the world has shrunk and time zones have eroded.

You can contact people wherever they are and it doesn't matter where you are, and you can do it at any time of the day. Some people no longer bother with a physical address; they find it too restricting as they embrace the virtual world.

The chief obstacle to the progress of the human race is the human race.
Don Marquis (1878–1937)

If you want to achieve more with your network, try using a simple achievement matrix to check your progress and refresh your strategic networking plan:

Step 1.   Review your contacts database and list your achievements and successes over the last month. How many new contacts have you added? How many existing contacts did you manage to reach? Were these virtual or physical exchanges?

Step 2. List the obstacles that you have overcome and those that are yet to be resolved. Was it a time-management issue? Did you attend a sufficient number of networking events? Have you increased your online network? If so, what method was most successful?

Step 3. Make a note of the action you will need to take to resolve the latest issues. Do you need to contact more people? If so how will you do this? Have you progressed certain connections as far as possible? Are you awaiting information from other people, which they promised you? Have you followed through with the information, introductions etc that you have offered people in your network?

Step 4. List the objectives for the next period. How many people do you wish to connect with by the end of the month? What percentage of these are existing contacts and how many are new introductions? Are your work-getting targets progressing according to plan?

Key point

Here's a checklist for developing powerful relationships.

Be transparent in your actions. Communicate with all sides as well as upwards and downwards. Network extensively to keep yourself well informed. Identify and watch the 'politicians'. Put yourself in other people's shoes. Anticipate and manage others' reactions. Be clearly good at your job.

Remember that every relationship is different. Without business contacts, preferably positive ones, you will make little progress. All your contacts are unique, some are demanding, others quite difficult, and some require understanding. Understanding them doesn't just make your relationship building easier; it is inherent to the whole process. Where there is no understanding how can a business relationship develop?

In essence the ingredients to successful networking are: being sincere and establishing trust (respecting your business contacts and your staff); and showing gratitude. Saying thank you costs you nothing and gains you much. If someone says 'Thank goodness we met,' treasure that moment. You may get testimonials from satisfied clients or recommenders, accept them and use them to lead to more. Persevere and all these relationships will flourish.

And finally... if you want to network successfully, you will remember the importance of these four words: curiosity (asking questions); generosity (giving to others); confidence (inspiring trust and showing respect); motivation (having a purpose). Remember, networking isn't about you – it's about *other people*.

With over 42 years of publishing, more than 80 million people have succeeded in business with thanks to **Kogan Page**

www.koganpage.com

KoganPage